The Two Witnesses Prepare the Bride

Patricia Baird Clark

The Two Witnesses Prepare the Bride

Patricia Baird Clark

Copyright © 2014 Patricia Baird Clark

ISBN 978-1-935018-76-6

PUBLISHED BY: Five Stones Publishing
A DIVISION OF: The International Localization Network
randy2905@gmail.com
ILNcenter.com

Without limiting the rights under copyright reserved above, no part of this publication may be reproduced, stored in or introduced into a retrieval system, or transmitted, in any form, or by any means (electronic, mechanical, photocopying, recording, or otherwise), without the prior written permission of the publisher.

Scriptures taken from the King James Version

www.HisPresenceOnline.org

Interior Design: Randall E. Johnson
Cover: Johnny Eckerman

Table of Contents

Dedication Page 3
  INTRODUCTION 7

CHAPTER ONE 9
  The Identity of the Two Witnesses 9
  John 9
  The Holy Spirit 10
  The Call to Preach 15
  The Altar 17
  The Court Without 19
  The Holy City 20
  Tread Under Foot 21
  Forty-Two Months 21
  The Period of Antichrist 23
  1260 days = 42 months 24

CHAPTER II 27
  The Two Olive Trees 27
  The Two Candlesticks 31
  Standing 33
  If Any Man 34
  Fire Out of Their Mouth 35
  No Rain 36
  Waters Turned to Blood 37
  Smiting the Earth with Plagues 37

CHAPTER III 41
  The Beast 41
  Dead Bodies 44
  Sodom and Egypt 44
  No Burial Permitted 46
  Our Testimony 47
  Rejoicing Over Their Deaths 50
  Three and a Half days 52
  Great Fear 53
  In a Cloud 54

CHAPTER IV 57
- A Great Earthquake 57
- The Woes... 60
- The Seventh Angel Sounds................................. 61
- The Twenty four Elders....................................... 64
- Sitting before God 65
- The Spiritual Mind Worships 66

CHAPTER V... 69
- Which Art 69
- Which Wast 71
- And Art to Come 73
- Our God Reigns 73
- The Angry Nations 74
- The Judgment of the Dead..................................77
- Judgment Comes Before Rewards 77
- Destroying the Earth 80
- The Day of the Lord 84
- The Temple Opened..85
- The Ark of His Testament 87
- Lightnings, Voices and Thunderings 87
- An Earthquake 88
- My Earthquake Experience 88
- Great Hail... 90

Appendix I 93
Appendix II Bible Study Questions 102

With gratitude and love to my husband, Stoner

The Two Witnesses Prepare the Bride

INTRODUCTION

It is early March in 2014. Our winter of extreme cold is hanging on with single digit temperatures and more snow in the forecast. At one point this winter there was snow on the ground in forty-nine of our fifty states with Florida being the only exception (USA Today). California, where we get 50% of our fruits and vegetables, is experiencing its worst drought in history. Orchards that were developed over decades are now dead or dying.

It takes only a little online research to learn that weather all over the world is being geoengineered. According to Dane Wigington head of GeoEngineering Watch,

> There is virtually no natural weather due to massive global climate engineering. The very essentials needed to sustain life on earth are being recklessly destroyed by these programs. This is not a topic that will begin to affect us in several years, but is now already causing massive animal and plant die off around the world, as well as human illness (Wigington).

This is not the only problem that is endangering our whole planet. The damaged Fukushima nuclear reactors in Japan have been pouring enormous amounts of radioactive materials into the atmosphere and the Pacific Ocean since March 11 2011, and there seems to be no end in sight. Governments worldwide are lying about the dangerous effects of the radiation so that their people are taking no precautions. Already there are increases of cancer and radiation induced diabetes seen in the areas most affected by the disaster… Japan, Hawaii, Alaska, Canada, Mexico, and the U.S. among others (Moret). Why are governments not warning their people? Because of Agenda 21, a UN mandate to kill off 90% of the world's population to "save" the planet.

These are only a few of the myriad problems facing us today any one of which could wipe out the lives of most living beings on our planet.

Where is our hope? Our hope is in God working through his church. No matter how weak and fragmented the church appears to be at this time, God is going to use it in ways that will astound the world. His people will have more power than the world has ever seen. This church will perform the "greater works" spoken of by Jesus in John 14:12.

However, first the church needs to be judged and cleansed. In its present condition, it looks no different than the world. God has been preparing a ministry to go forth into the churches in the end times that will bring the church into the unity of faith and doctrine. Many will come into the fullness of Christ. This will only come about as the ministry of the two witnesses goes out into the churches with a powerful word and demonstration of God's power and judgment that will prepare his church to be the bride who, when joined with the Bridegroom, will transform the world and usher in God's kingdom.

As we shall see in the interpretation of Revelation 11 offered in this book, the churches will only be open to receive this powerful ministry when something cataclysmic takes place that will totally stun the church and her leaders to the point that they will be willing to lay down their pet doctrines and false beliefs that have kept the church divided and arguing for centuries.

God spent four thousand years preparing humanity for the first coming of Christ. He has spent the last two thousand years preparing us for the second coming. This preparation will be in full-throttle acceleration as the ministers, who have spent a lifetime in preparation by the hand of God, move forth into the powerful ministry reserved for the church of the end times.

CHAPTER ONE

The Identity of the Two Witnesses

First we must identify who these two witnesses are. Upon this disclosure the rest of this revelation hangs in the balance. They appear first in verse three,

> *Rev 11:3 And I will give power unto my two witnesses, and they shall prophesy a thousand two hundred and threescore days, clothed in sackcloth.*

There have been many suppositions as to just who these two persons are. Some have said Enoch and Elijah; some Elijah and Moses; and others possibly Zerubbabel and Joshua. These possibilities have been offered based on a literal interpretation of this Revelation passage.

My interpretation is allegorical rather than literal with the allegorical type being defined by the Bible itself. Numbers are interpreted according to their spiritual meaning rather than their strict numerical value. I would like to offer the following reasons for my understanding about the identity of these two witnesses.

The first thing I did in researching was to find every scripture in the Bible with the word "witness" in it. There were two persons who stood out as being most identified as witnesses. These were John the Baptist and the Holy Spirit.

John

> *There was a man sent from God, whose name was John. The same came for a witness, to bear witness of the Light, that all men through him might believe (John 1:6, 7).*

The Holy Spirit

But when the Comforter is come, whom I will send unto you from the Father, even the Spirit of truth, which proceedeth from the Father, he shall testify of me (John 15:26).

As I pondered this, it occurred to me that it was John the Baptist who prepared the way for the first coming of Christ. It would be appropriate for a John the Baptist type ministry to prepare the way for the second coming of Christ. I could see several similarities. Also the witnesses minister similarly to the way Elijah ministered and John the Baptist was compared to Elijah by Jesus (Matt 11:14; 17:11, 12).

Later on in Revelation the beast kills the two witnesses. Obviously the Holy Spirit cannot be killed, and John Baptist already died so he couldn't be killed either. My answer to this is that the two witnesses represent a great ministry that will go forth in the end times. It is the ministry that will be killed and then resurrected not the individuals themselves.

If we truly understand God's ways, then we know that the principle of death and resurrection is necessary in any life, individual or corporate, if it is to be God-infused. Only a person who is dead to self can be trusted by God not to misuse his power. I believe this is why we see such a lack of God's power in most churches today. People are too full of self to be entrusted with God's power. It would only corrupt them and wind up being misused.

Moses was a man whose ministry went into death and then resurrection. He thought he would rescue the Hebrews when he was a prince of Egypt and killed an Egyptian man who was abusing a Hebrew. God removed him from this position…a position that for all appearances looked like the perfect place for a deliverer to be. But God's ways are not our ways. God removed him from his position and took him into the wilderness for forty years where he was greatly humbled. After this preparation, God had a man he could use because Moses knew he could do nothing apart from God. God delivered the Hebrews his way and it was done with a demonstration of his great power and glory through a man who put no trust in himself but only moved at

God's direction under God's authority. No man would receive credit for what only God could do.

God does not need for Moses or any other biblical figure to come back to earth to do another great ministry. God only needs humble vessels who have been willing to spend time on the backside of the desert with God being divested of self to such an extent that God can use them even as he used Moses.

Just as individual Christians need to die to self, so do corporate Christian bodies. The strongest church is usually a church that has suffered difficulties that to all appearances killed it, but it rose up out of the ashes to become a strong church. The church historically began with great manifestations of God's power. The church weakened and went through the centuries referred to as the Dark Ages when Catholicism reigned and the true light of Christ remained alive in only a relatively small remnant. With the Reformation, the church began to rise again out of the ashes. Ultimately the church of the end times will have greater power than the First Century church but only after the death and resurrection of the historical church has been fully accomplished.

Seeing this principle of death and resurrection in the individual lives of biblical characters, in history and in lives of persons living today, it seems quite in keeping with God's ways for the ministry of the two witnesses to also follow this principle. This is why I believe the ministry of the two witnesses is killed, not the witnesses themselves.

In interpreting Revelation we need to remember that it is an allegory. In allegory certain individual biblical characters often represent groups of people who have similar characteristics or a similar call. For example, it is not unusual to think of Moses as representing a present day ministry that saves people out of the world (Egypt) and helps them through the difficulties of their lives (wilderness wanderings). A Joshua type ministry today is one that brings people into maturity and helps them enter into the fullness of Christ (cross over Jordan into the Promised Land).

The literal interpretations of the two witnesses most frequently offered raise many questions. Why would God have to bring people back from the dead to do the work of the two witnesses when he has many Christians alive on earth now who are willing vessels waiting to do whatever ministry the Lord desires? How could just two men minister to the billions of people in all the nations on the planet? Why would God allow his witnesses to be killed if they had already died once and it is appointed to man once to die?

It is true that Elijah and Enoch had different exits from this earth but still that raises many questions such as: How would men who had lived in pre-modern times deal with seeing airplanes, automobiles, cell phones, computers and all the electrical devices we now take for granted? How could they minister to people whose lives and culture are based on the history of all those who have preceded them for thousands of years? Perhaps we think of major biblical characters as having special abilities that people today don't possess rather than understanding they were just vessels that the Holy Spirit worked through to accomplish his purposes on earth.

It is important to consider what Jesus said about John the Baptist: "And if ye will receive it, this is Elias, which was for to come" (Matt 11:14). Jesus was saying here that the same anointing and Spirit were upon John that had been on Elijah. To say that Elijah had literally come back to earth in John would reinforce the false concept of reincarnation. We need to understand that it is no different in these end times. It is the anointing upon the witnesses that is important, not who the persons are in and of themselves. They are human vessels who have chosen to totally submit their will to the will of the Father to do whatever he directs.

Now I want to put this together with Malachi 4 where the Lord tells us that the great and dreadful day of the Lord will not come until Elijah comes. We know that Elijah did come in the ministry of John the Baptist but there are two things cited in Malachi 4 that definitely point to this happening again in the present modern age in which we live. Let's look first at Malachi:

> For, behold, the day cometh, that shall burn as an oven; and all the proud, yea, and all that do wickedly, shall be stubble: and the day that cometh shall burn them up, saith the LORD of hosts, that it shall leave them neither root nor branch.(Malachi 4:1)

There are two ways of interpreting this...literally and figuratively...and both are accurate. First the literal interpretation: This has to be speaking about nuclear holocaust. Not only do we face the threat of almost sure nuclear war but also the radioactive damage that comes from nuclear power plant accidents. I won't go into this in detail here because I do so towards the end of this book, but suffice it to say much of our world is even now burning like an oven because of nuclear radiation. There are large portions of our planet being made uninhabitable right now because of the greed and wickedness of evil men who control others.

With radiation poisoning a person literally burns up from the inside out. The cells of the body are agitated by the radiation causing the atoms in the cells to move more rapidly and heat up. Cells break and the agitated atoms move out to damage other cells. There is no known way to stop it. "At extremely high doses, radiation causes cell death, through a process called thermalization, which basically cooks a cell from the inside out" (wiseGEEK).

This is what is described in Malachi 4:1. This is what it means to burn as an oven. If you are not convinced, consider the last words of this verse: "that it shall leave them neither root nor branch." Root would refer to heredity which has everything to do with our DNA. In radiation poisoning, the DNA strands are damaged irreparably thus leaving us with no root. There will be no branch on the family tree because radiation damage causes sterility. If children are born, they are often severely deformed. Once the DNA is damaged, there will be no repairing it in future generations even if there are any. The Chernobyl nuclear power plant disaster caused over a million cancer deaths and many deformed babies. You can find the truth, complete with pictures, on the Internet. We have been lied to.

And now for my *spiritual* interpretation of Malachi 4:1: In these end times in all of us who love and serve Jesus, God is going to burn up our sin nature with all its pride leaving it neither root nor branch. When God does this, it will be completely gone. This is one of the rewards reserved for the church of the end times. When the carnal nature is gone, there will be no sickness and we will walk in victory over all our enemies as prophesied in the next two verses in Malachi 4:

> But unto you that fear my name shall the Sun of righteousness arise with healing in his wings; and ye shall go forth, and grow up as calves of the stall. And ye shall tread down the wicked; for they shall be ashes under the soles of your feet in the day that I shall do this, saith the LORD of hosts (Mal 4:2, 3).

In the last two verses of Malachi 4 the Lord promises,

> I will send you Elijah the prophet before the coming of the great and dreadful day of the LORD. And he shall turn the heart of the fathers to the children, and the heart of the children to their fathers, lest I come and smite the earth with a curse (Mal 4:5, 6).

"Today, one-third of American children – a total of 15 million – are being raised without a father" (Andersen). This has a profound effect on the lives of these children making it difficult for them to have a relationship with God the Father or to find any anchor for their life. Children raised without a father or strong father-figure are much more likely to get involved in crime, drug abuse, immorality, low academic performance, and suffer from depression, rage, and suicidal tendencies. Truly this is a symptom of the times in which we live and there is a desperate need for a powerful move of God to rectify the damage done in the lives of adults and children alike who have suffered this deprivation.

Based on all the above, I believe the two witnesses are this John the Baptist Company of believers and the Holy Spirit… an indefinite number of people filled with the Holy Spirit who will minister powerfully to the church of the end times. Every verse in the rest of this chapter falls perfectly in line with this interpretation to reveal the particulars about this ministry.

God has been quietly preparing this group of people unbeknownst to the world or even the church at large. They are like the stones that were prepared underground for Solomon's temple:

> *And the house, when it was in building, was built of stone made ready before it was brought thither: so that there was neither hammer nor ax nor any tool of iron heard in the house, while it was in building (1 Kings 6:7).*

These ministers have been in the wilderness with God where every motive, thought and action has been judged by God. Only those who are dead to self will be allowed to be in this august group of ministers. God will only entrust his great power and anointing to those who will use it exclusively at his leading. This will require total surrender and death to self and the world. Their love and devotion to Jesus will allow him to manifest himself through them. This ministry will prepare the church to be the pure, spotless bride that Jesus is coming for. The same standards that have been required of the John the Baptist Company will also be required of every believer who desires to be the bride.

Now that we understand who the two witnesses are, let's begin our study with verse one of Revelation 11.

> *Rev 11:1 And there was given me a reed like unto a rod: and the angel stood, saying, Rise, and measure the temple of God, and the altar, and them that worship therein.*

The Call to Preach

If we were to take this verse literally, we would think there is a physical building someplace called a temple whose measurements God desires to know. However, our God is not interested in any architectural structure built by men. He is interested in the temple built of living stones that he is building and that he is coming to inhabit. So this is not the measuring of a literal building but the measuring of people. The church will be measured and judged corporately (temple) and also individually (them that worship therein).

If we look at this verse in the context of the previous verse in Revelation 10 we learn more about how the measuring will be done.

> *Rev 10:11 And he said unto me, Thou must prophesy again before many peoples, and nations, and tongues, and kings.*

In my interpretation of the book of Revelation, each chapter flows into the next in a flow of context that reveals believers in the end times coming into the fullness of Christ. If we look at these chapters for their outward interpretation, we will see in many places great, divine judgment coming upon the world. If we view these same passages inwardly and allegorically, we can see a progressive working of the Holy Spirit in believers to rid them of their sin nature, draw them into a deeper relationship with God and awaken in them the spiritual side of their being that died (as in all humankind) at the time of the fall.

To prophesy, *propheteuo*, is to speak under divine inspiration. Since this word is in the verse directly preceding Revelation 11:1, we can rightly assume that contextually it will have some bearing on this verse.

The temple is comprised of people. The thing that God wants to measure in the people is their hearts. God uses his Word to reveal our hearts. Therefore, the "reed like unto a rod" has to be the preaching of the Word. Reed, in Greek, is *kalamos,* and is defined as being a pen. "My tongue is the pen of a ready writer" (Psa 45:1), immediately comes to mind.

As these ministers preach the word of God it will cause people's hearts to be measured by their response to the preaching. Some of them will like the preaching. They will take it to heart, and grow and thrive on it. Others listening to the word preached will not like it. They will harden their hearts and disagree with it. They might even get angry. The word of God always demands a verdict. Therefore, even a passive response to the proclamation of the word is tantamount to rejecting it. This is how preaching measures the true temple of God which is the hearts of the people.

This principle is seen in John 6 where Jesus told his disciples that if they would eat his flesh and drink his blood they would have eternal life. This was difficult for all to understand and some left him at that point as seen in John 6:66, "From that time many of his disciples went back, and walked no more with him." But the twelve remained even though they did not understand at the time what Jesus meant. Peter spoke for the group saying they would remain faithful to him because he alone had the words of life. Jesus, who knew men's hearts, knew that even among those who remained there was one who would not follow but would betray him.

We have seen this principle displayed in the church down through the ages and also in this present age. People gather as Christians to worship and grow together in Christ, but it is often not long before there arises some difference over interpretation of the Word or some other issue and separation comes. In these end times we will see the church purified and perfected as the separations occur until there remains a remnant that truly walks in holiness.

The Altar

The most important word these ministers will preach is the message of the cross which is represented by the altar. All Christians understand the historical cross…that Jesus died on the cross and took their sins upon himself so they could be forgiven. The altar is a place of sacrifice. Jesus placed his own life on the altar as a sacrifice that we might have access to God because of his great love. If we love God in return, we must also place our lives on the cross. Jesus made that abundantly clear when he said,

> *If any man will come after me, let him deny himself, and take up his cross daily, and follow me. For whosoever will save his life shall lose it: but whosoever will lose his life for my sake, the same shall save it (Luke 9:23, 24).*

We must die to self that Jesus can live his life through us. This has been a very unpopular message in the modern church. The popular message of prosperity has built large, "successful" ministries, but the life and power of God has often been absent in these churches. It is the preaching of the cross, the message that we must die to self and let Christ live in us, that brings power and glory to the church.

This is how the altar will be measured. Are we willing to die to self, or are we going to try to use God to get what we want? Only those willing to die will be allowed to move ahead with God into his kingdom in these end times.

Both the church corporately and individuals have to make this decision. The corporate church's decision to follow Christ to the death will most likely result in just that. It takes money to pay for a church building, the utilities, church programs, and the salaries of the ministers. This is totally dependent upon the giving of the members. If an uncompromising message of the cross is preached, there will be members who don't like it. They won't like it because they don't want to give up their self life to follow Christ. They want to have their cake and eat it too, so to speak. They will challenge the minister who, if he will not compromise, will be asked to leave or they will leave. Losing a portion of the congregation usually makes it impossible to pay the bills. Therefore, to keep the corporate group intact, many a minister and church council have been willing to compromise to keep the peace. It is easy to forget that Jesus said,

Think not that I am come to send peace on earth: I came not to send peace, but a sword. For I am come to set a man at variance against his father, and the daughter against her mother, and the daughter-in-law against her mother-in-law. And a man's foes shall be they of his own household. He that loveth father or mother more than me is not worthy of me: and he that loveth son or daughter more than me is not worthy of me. And he that taketh not his cross, and followeth after me, is not worthy of me (Matt 10:34-38).

This is true in natural families and also true in church families. If we are to come into the fullness of Christ, this cannot be avoided. It has been our experience, after over forty years in pastoral ministry, that the only way to be free to follow Jesus no matter what, is to be free of any denominational ties and to meet in homes. Denominational overseers are under the gun to produce bigger churches and more churches. We were told that healthy sheep have lambs. If your church is not growing numerically, it is not a healthy church. We have found that to be absolutely not true. There are different seasons in God. Sometimes God is maturing and purifying a group of people before he adds to it. We felt pressured by overseers to conform to their standards and that if we did not, we were failures. It is incredibly freeing to be released from that. The whole hierarchical system of leadership is a holdover from the Constantinian influence that dictated church hegemony for centuries.

Verse and Interpretation

Rev 11:1 And there was given me a reed like unto a rod: and the angel stood, saying, Rise, and measure the temple of God, and the altar, and them that worship therein.

There are persons who have received a call from God to go forth and preach in the churches (Rev 10:11). They are told that their words (reed) will measure the hearts of the people (temple) both corporately and individually. Persons will have to decide whether or not they are willing to die to self (altar) in order to follow Christ.

* * * * * * * * *

Rev 11:2 But the court which is without the temple leave out, and measure it not; for it is given unto the Gentiles: and the holy city shall they tread under foot forty and two months.

The Court Without

This reminds me of the tabernacle in the wilderness. There was an outer court where any Israelite could go to bring his sacrifice to be slain on the brazen altar by the priest, but only the Levitical priests could enter the holy place to minister before the Lord. The Bible tells us that all believers are called to be priests to minister to the Lord. If we remain in the outer court we have chosen to have a form of religion and have rejected the true essence of Christianity which is a relationship with God. Therefore I believe the outer court represents those who have chosen to follow "another gospel" (Gal 1:6). Jesus provided the way for all true believers to fully enter in to the presence of God through his cross and resurrection. Therefore, to remain in the outer court as a New Covenant believer is to deny the efficacious work of Christ at the cross. It is to follow another gospel.

This outer court church is comprised of people who gather together in the name of religion. They may consider themselves Christian, but they don't really believe the gospel. They have compromised. They have taken certain scriptures and said, "Well, that's not true. We don't believe that." Other scriptures they over-emphasize or twist the meaning into something devoid of scriptural truth.

The message here is, Don't go and preach there because "it is given to the Gentiles." Gentiles represent unbelievers in type. Since these people are not really believers, it would make no sense to go into those churches and preach the gospel to them because they already know what the Bible says, and they have rejected the truth. Therefore, the Lord is not sending the witnesses there.

The Holy City

In both the Old and New Testaments, Jerusalem is the holy city. Jerusalem is a type of the true church. In Isaiah the Lord prophesies that his church will someday come to perfection:

> *Awake, awake; put on thy strength, O Zion; put on thy beautiful garments, O Jerusalem, the holy city: for henceforth there shall no more come into thee the uncircumcised and the unclean (Isa 52:1).*

There is a part of our being that is spiritual in nature that went to sleep, so to speak, at the time of the fall. In the end times God will awaken this part of us and in so doing will enable us to have a much closer walk with God. At that time we will put on our beautiful garment which is Christ. This will be the presence of God that will perceptibly come upon us. This will be discussed in much more detail towards the end of this book.

When the church rises to this level of spiritual maturity, they will have the discernment to determine the difference between true believers and those that just come to church for social reasons or perhaps are even in the enemy's camp. We are naïve if we do not believe the enemy of our souls will send his own into the midst of the church to cause strife and division. The tares and wheat have been growing together throughout the ages but at the time of the end they will be separated. The preaching of the two witnesses will be such that the deceivers will be exposed and will either leave or be converted. God will have a purified church.

In Revelation we see the true church finally perfected:

> And I John saw the holy city, new Jerusalem, coming down from God out of heaven, prepared as a bride adorned for her husband (Rev 21:2).

The work of the two witnesses will be to prepare this bride. No matter what the church looks like at this point, God will have his pure, spotless bride.

Tread Under Foot

The outer court church will persecute the true church. It has always been so since the inception of the church. At that time Jews persecuted Christians. Now, in America, pseudo Christians persecute the true Christians. In other places in the world, Muslims are persecuting Christians. Often governments persecute Christians. I recently read the book, *The Heavenly Man*, about Brother Yun and the persecution of the true church in China by both the false church and the government. They recognize that God has used the persecution to mature and cleanse them. Those of us in the West will also see severe persecution as not only the false church but also our own government and those of other religious persuasions will come against us.

Forty-Two Months

We see in this verse that the outer court church is persecuting the true church for a period of forty-two months. I see this as not a literal length of time but a spiritual understanding regarding time. According to E. W. Bullinger, forty-two is the number of the Antichrist, with Antichrist representing that which opposes the will of God. He bases this on this verse we are currently examining but also the following:

- Forty-two stages of Israel's wanderings mark their conflict with the will of God.
- Forty-two young men mocked the ascension of Elijah to Elisha, (2 Kings 2:23, 24).

- It is the product of 6 times 7 with 6 being the number of man in enmity against God and 7 being the number of God's perfect will (Bullinger, 268).

Antichrist is mentioned five times in Scripture, twice in the following verse:

Little children, it is the last time: and as ye have heard that antichrist shall come, even now are there many antichrists; whereby we know that it is the last time (1 John 2:18).

We can see by this passage that the Antichrist spirit was active in the very beginning of the church. The words "the last time" refer to the past two thousand years. This confirms what many already know and that is that God has been preparing his church for the second coming of Christ for two thousand years. Christians today have been enabled to learn and stand based on the contributions and testimonies of those who have preceded us. In all ages the true Christians have been watching and believing that at any time the Lord would return. So we see here that this has been something that has been ongoing for many years.

The remaining references to the Antichrist are in 1 John and also 2 John. These reveal that the Antichrist denies the Father and the Son and also that Jesus came in the flesh. These, then, are characteristics of the Antichrist spirit that have been in operation for the past two thousand years. However, in these end times we will see a great intensification of the activities of this spirit.

Verse and Interpretation

Rev 11:2 But the court which is without the temple leave out, and measure it not; for it is given unto the Gentiles: and the holy city shall they tread under foot forty and two months.

Don't go to preach in the churches that believe a false gospel (temple without). It has been given to the unbelievers who have rejected the true gospel (Gentiles). They will persecute the true church (holy city) during the time of the Antichrist until the Lord comes (forty-two months).

* * * * * * * * *

Rev 11:3 And I will give power unto my two witnesses, and they shall prophesy a thousand two hundred and threescore days, clothed in sackcloth.

The Period of Antichrist

The ministry spoken of here is not comprised of just two individuals but of the Holy Spirit and a John the Baptist Company of believers. This ministry will be very similar to the ministry of John the Baptist. He was in the wilderness even as this company of believers has been in the spiritual wilderness being prepared by God for this ministry. People going out to John the Baptist in the wilderness were asking questions as though there was some desperation in their lives.

Those coming to the two witnesses for ministry will also be experiencing times of trial and testing in their own lives. People, particularly in America, have most often been quite casual about their faith in Christ. It will become apparent to all Christians and many who are not Christians that their only hope for surviving the disasters coming against us is in God.

The two witnesses are clothed in sackcloth. Sackcloth is a type of humility, and humility will be a major characteristic of these ministers. Jesus Christ was a very humble man, and these ministers will be very much like Jesus. These humble people will do only what the Lord tells them to do. They will be filled with the Holy Spirit and the words they speak will be the words of God.

Even though this ministry has been going on in some form for two thousand years, it is going to be greatly intensified in the end times. There will be greater power and we will see amazing things coming from the true church in these end times. Even though I've said the Antichrist spirit has been here for two thousand years, we are going to see some things that have not been seen before. There are things about this ministry that have been hidden beneath the surface of Revelation 11 because they were to be known only by the church of the end times. Churches of other eras could not walk in the power and anointing that will be seen here because it has been reserved for those who will face the greatest evil of all time and at the same time enter into the fullness of Christ.

The word *prophecy* in this verse speaks of the ministry that is going to go forth from these ministers. It is going to be supernatural ministry. They are going to speak forth pure words from God. They will be able to tell people what is in their hearts and some of what God has planned for them in their future. I believe they will be able to see into the hearts of men and women and be able to point out to them obstacles lodged in their hearts that are prohibiting them from progressing in their relationship with God. They are going to be able to identify sin in a person's life so the person can be aware of it and repent.

It is very difficult to know our own heart. I know I don't know my own heart, and many times God has pointed out to me something in my heart I needed to repent of that I had no idea was there. The ministers are going to be able to do this because God wants to get his bride ready for the Lord Jesus Christ, the Bridegroom. This ministry is going to be very powerful. It is going to help people quickly grow and mature, identify their sin and repent and come into the perfection that God wants for the bride of Christ in the end times.

As we finish this verse let's look at the number of days they are said to prophecy… a thousand two hundred and threescore days. A little math reveals that…

1260 days = 42 months

As stated earlier, 42 is the number of Antichrist. I do not believe it is a literal period of time but rather a spiritual understanding of time that is needful here. E.W. Bullinger states that 42 "is significant of the working out of man's opposition to God." So the period of time given in this verse is indicative of the period of time necessary for God to accomplish what he intends to do through the two witnesses. Even true believers have some opposition to God in their hearts. Through the ministry of the two witnesses, this will be identified so the people can repent, die to self and with God's help progress rapidly into the fullness of Christ.

Verse and Interpretation

Rev 11:3 And I will give power unto my two witnesses, and they shall prophesy a thousand two hundred and threescore days, clothed in sackcloth.

I will give power to the John the Baptist Company filled with the Holy Spirit (two witnesses). They will preach my word (prophesy) during the period of time marked by the Antichrist spirit (1,260 days). They will be very humble people (sackcloth).

* * * * * * * * *

CHAPTER II

Rev 11:4 (a) These are the two olive trees, (b) and the two candlesticks (c) standing before the God of the earth.

The Two Olive Trees

The two olive trees represent the Holy Spirit and the John the Baptist Company of believers. They are two yet they are one in testimony and one in relationship. These ministers are filled with the Holy Spirit and the Holy Spirit is ministering through them to prepare the body of Christ to be that pure, spotless bride.

Sometimes in Scripture men are referred to as being trees. John the Baptist compared men to trees. We see this in Luke 3:9:

And now also the ax is laid unto the root of the trees: every tree therefore which bringeth not forth good fruit is hewn down, and cast into the fire. (Luke 3:9)

John the Baptist was not talking about literal fruit trees here with roots that go down into the ground and branches and leaves and blossoms and fruit. He was talking about human beings, and his ministry was a ministry of judgment. It was a ministry of judgment then and it will be a ministry of judgment coming forth from the John the Baptist ministers in the end times. In the account we have of John the Baptist in the Scriptures, he was somewhat harsh in his preaching. For example when speaking to the scribes and Pharisees he said, "Ye serpents, ye generation of vipers, how can ye escape the damnation of hell? (Mat 23:33).

The preaching of judgment going forth in the end times doesn't necessarily have to be that abrasive in the way the ministers speak to people, but it is a ministry that convicts people's hearts. The witnesses won't necessarily have to stand up and preach hellfire and damnation (although they could do that), but anything they say will convict people's hearts because the Holy Spirit is moving through them. The only way God is going to have a pure bride without spot or wrinkle is if we identify our sins and repent of our sins and begin to live righteously before the Lord. This ministry is going to help the church do this.

This John the Baptist ministry is not intentionally preaching in order to judge people, but the anointing that is on them judges them. It's like no matter what they teach, no matter what they preach, it brings conviction into people's hearts. Conviction forces them to make decisions. Some go with God and some refuse. This separates the people and division takes place in the church.

When my husband and I started in pastoral ministry in 1970, we just wanted to build a nice little church where everybody loved one another and helped each other. But it wasn't like that. We would go into a church and it would grow in numbers. People would be maturing in the Lord. To all outward appearances, our churches were prosperous. But there were always those that opposed us. They would build their army, so to speak, and come against us and try to run us out of the church.

We would pray, Lord, can't we just have a nice little church? We don't want a mega church… just something big enough that we can support missionaries and help our community. We want to help people be all they can be in Christ. Why can't we build something that lasts?

We did have churches like that, but powerful opposition would come against us every time. My ministry of rescuing abused people from satanic cults that began in 1992 made our churches a prime target for curses and aroused fear in many Christians. In my naivety I thought they would join us in the fight, but I learned the hard way that few Christians want to join the fight, much less hang around where it is being waged! This is very sad because it is good preparation for what we will face in the great battles of the end times that are even now beginning.

We didn't realize we were in training to be part of the John the Baptist Company. We knew we were to minister in the end times but did not realize the importance of separation or that it was necessary to cleanse the church. It was like everything we preached or taught caused people to get convicted and they would either move forward with the Lord or they would get angry and direct their anger at us.

The two witnesses are described as being two olive trees. It is from olives when they are pressed that we get oil that is used in anointing oil. These trees are a type of the anointing of the Holy Spirit. The fact that these are trees rather than merely the oil itself suggests that the anointing is flowing out from God himself and there is no end to this anointing. They will not run out of oil or olives from which to make the oil because the tree itself is a living thing and produces continually. It is perpetual. It is constantly upon them and flowing out through them.

I don't believe anointing is necessarily something that is discernable. It is not identified by certain inflections of the voice or actions of the body which many have interpreted as meaning anointing. There are actually some people who believe the preacher is under the anointing of God if he runs around on the platform or uses an affected voice when he speaks. Some ministers are said to be under the anointing when they put an "a" sound at the end of every word. The anointing is not even that miracles take place in the service. The Devil can cause miraculous things to happen.

The anointing is the presence, power and activity of the Holy Spirit on a person's life. It is placed there by God to accomplish that for which this person has been called. In the next few verses of Revelation 11 we will see how this particular anointing manifests through the witnesses.

Just as the first John the Baptist preached a convicting word that judged people's hearts, so also will this end time John the Baptist company preach a word that convicts. It is not necessarily their intention to do so, but the anointing on them will cause conviction to come in the hearts of those who hear them. If there is to be a perfect bride, then that which is not perfect will have to be divided from that which is perfect and discarded. This will be ongoing in individual hearts and also in corporate groups. Only through conviction and separation can there be perfection.

People who have this anointing usually don't recognize it. They don't understand why when they are living a godly life, giving their all to the church, doing everything they can to help people and preach a good word, that people get upset with them, criticize them and leave the church. They just don't understand why this continually happens. It may well be that they have this John the Baptist anointing and that God intends for there to be separation.

There are some believers that are going to go all the way with God and are going to come into the fullness of Christ and be that pure, spotless bride. There are others that just aren't going to do it. They are going to live for themselves. They want things their way. When you talk about the cross and dying to self, they're just going to go to some other church that preaches you can have what you say and that God wants us all to be rich and prosperous.

Many preachers don't understand this. If they understood it, it could save them a lot of grief. We didn't realize all those years ago when we started out in ministry that we were part of this John the Baptist Company. We did not understand that the ministry coming forth from us was supposed to cause separation. If we had known this, it would not have been such a devastating event when the church split and therefore did not grow in numbers. In fact, I remember one time when our church was losing people that the Lord clearly said to me, "I didn't bring you here to build a big church. I brought you here to build you."

Certainly there can be a lot of growth and maturing happening in the lives of these ministers if they respond to their disappointments the way God would have them respond when opposition arises around them and people blame them for doing things they didn't do.

In the early 1980s when my husband and I had recently experienced a church split, we were extremely discouraged. We had a friend in a nearby city who was the associate pastor of a large church. They had asked my husband to come and preach at their Wednesday night service. We were in the car on the way there and in my husband's great discouragement he said, "I don't know why anybody would want me to come and minister to their congregation. I feel like John the Baptist. I feel like I'm a prisoner. All these other men can go out here and have successful ministries and build up their churches, but I'm just a prisoner."

Before my husband preached, there was a worship service with the singing of several choruses. After the last song when everyone was quietly standing, a prophetic word boomed forth from a man we had never seen before. These were his words:

> There are those standing here tonight who feel like a prisoner, but I want you to know that the chains that bind you are not the chains of the Devil. You are not in these chains because you have done anything wrong. These are the chains of trial and testing. Be patient just a little while longer and I will break your chains, and when I do, the angels will sing and there is going to be glory.

This took place in the early 1980s and it is now 2014 as of this writing. I have learned over time that God's concept of "a little while longer" and mine differ significantly! It was many years before we had a church that was what we thought a church should be, but God had a lot of work to do in us before we could have that kind of a church. He had to change our whole understanding of what church is. We were very broken people. We did not know we were being prepared to be part of the John the Baptist Company even though my husband said he felt like John the Baptist in prison. But God was faithful and he took us through what we had to go through and now we have a very wonderful church. It is a house church. It is a small church, but it is a marvelous church and God is doing amazing things in our midst. We no longer feel that we are bound in chains but have yet to hear the angels sing.

The Two Candlesticks

The second part of Rev 11:4 says the two witnesses are "the two candlesticks standing before the God of the earth." My spiritual interpretation for the candlesticks comes from the Old Testament:

> *The spirit of man is the candle of the Lord, searching all the inward parts of the belly (Prov 20:27).*

The Hebrew word for spirit used here is *neshamah*. Of the 505 times spirit is mentioned in the Bible, only two times is this word *neshamah* used. *Ruwach* is by far the most common Hebrew word used for spirit. The Holy Spirit must have chosen this particular word for a special reason.

According to Gesenius, *neshamah* should be understood in Prov 20:27 as meaning "mind" (Gesenius). It also means "divine inspiration" and "intellect." Putting all these together…mind, divine inspiration, spirit, and intellect…I believe that *neshamah* represents our spiritual mind. Two candlesticks would be the spiritual mind of the person and the mind of Holy Spirit together.

The words the John the Baptist company of ministers speak are coming out of their spiritual mind in union with the Holy Spirit. This is a picture of what takes place under the anointing. The words of the Holy Spirit come into their spirit and then they speak words of divine inspiration that are straight from God. This is nothing like "channeling" that is done by demons speaking through people. This is coming out of human hearts and minds that are so one with Christ in love and purpose that the Lord can speak his words through them to his people. Major Ian Thomas says regarding Jesus,

> On the first day of Pentecost He returned, not this time to be with them externally--clothed with that sinless humanity that God had prepared for Him, being conceived of the Holy Spirit in the womb of Mary--but now to be in them, imparting to them His own divine nature, clothing Himself with their humanity, so that they each became "members in particular" of a new, corporate body through which Christ expressed Himself to the world of their day (Thomas, 14, 15).

The words preached under this anointing are searching the inward parts of the bellies, meaning the inner hearts of the people who are listening to their preaching. The Hebrew word for "belly" is *beten*, and it can also be translated "womb." The womb is the matrix out of which everything else flows. As Jesus said in *Luke 6:45*:

> A good man out of the good treasure of his heart bringeth forth that which is good; and an evil man out of the evil

treasure of his heart bringeth forth that which is evil: for of the abundance of the heart his mouth speaketh.

Jesus made it clear that good and evil are matters of the heart. The preaching of the witnesses will reveal what is in people's hearts. So we see here in verse four of Revelation 11 that their spiritual mind united with the mind of Christ is a lamp, or a candlestick of spiritual illumination that exposes what is in people's hearts. People will not be able to hear this preaching without being exposed in some way regarding what is really in their heart.

Standing

The two witnesses are standing before the God of all the earth. This reminds me of Elijah who, when confronting Ahab and prophesying about a great drought, said he was standing before the Lord.

> *And Elijah the Tishbite, who was of the inhabitants of Gilead, said unto Ahab, As the LORD God of Israel liveth, before whom I stand, there shall not be dew nor rain these years, but according to my word (1 Ki 17:1).*

The phrase, standing before God, means that they are standing in the authority of God. Whatever they say will be enforced by Almighty God because they are speaking God's words not their own. Elijah knew that Almighty God was backing up the words he spoke to Ahab because he stood before God. He knew these words were not his own but were from God.

Verse and Interpretation

Rev 11:4 These are the two olive trees, and the two candlesticks standing before the God of the earth.

The ministries filled with the Holy Spirit that are called to prepare the church for the second coming of Christ have an unceasing anointing continually flowing forth (two olive trees). Their spiritual mind united with the mind of Christ (two candlesticks) is a lamp that exposes what is in people's hearts. Whatever they say will be enforced by Almighty God because they are speaking God's words not their own (standing before God).

* * * * * * * * *

> Rev 11:5 And if any man will hurt them, fire proceedeth out of their mouth, and devoureth their enemies: and if any man will hurt them, he must in this manner be killed.

Next we are going to look at the powers these ministers have. Fire comes forth out of their mouths to kill their enemies. They can shut up the sky so it doesn't rain, turn the waters to blood and smite the earth with plagues. As we look at these powers according to my interpretation, with the two witnesses representing a ministry preparing the church for the second coming of Christ, we will see that this all fits together perfectly.

Some of the powers I just named here remind me of Old Testament characters. Elijah for when he called fire down from heaven and also when he told Ahab it would not rain for three and a half years. I also thought of Moses who turned the waters to blood and smote the earth with plagues. What we see literally in the Old Testament will have a spiritual counterpart in the New Testament. I would like to share now what I believe the spiritual counterpart would be in this John the Baptist ministry that is preparing the way for Christ. I do not believe that the people involved in this ministry are literally going to kill anybody, or that they are going to have literal fire coming out of their mouth. So there has to be a spiritual meaning here.

If Any Man

The word "man" is not in the Greek, so a better translation would be, "And if any will hurt them…" This is confirmed in Part B where once again the word "man" is not in the Greek. However, we can assume that "man" would be understood in this passage. According to the early Church Fathers, "men" allegorically represent understandings. Therefore, I believe what is opposing them here are certain understandings held by church people that are false and would be used to come against what the ministers are preaching. It is this sort of thing that has kept the church divided and weak. People just can't agree on basic doctrine.

However, this will change under the anointed preaching of the John the Baptist Company. There will be separation and a pure church will remain although it may be considerably smaller than before. Then the Lord can bring in new converts who will not be misled by false understandings or upset by conflicts within the church.

Fire Out of Their Mouth

Our understanding of the fire that comes from their mouths is found in Jeremiah:

> *Wherefore thus saith the LORD God of hosts, Because ye speak this word, behold, I will make my words in thy mouth fire, and this people wood, and it shall devour them (Jer 5:14).*

The preaching coming forth from the witnesses will be so powerful that no false understanding or doctrine (men) will be able to stand against it. These false beliefs won't stand a chance when confronted with the words and wisdom (fire) coming forth from the mouths of the witnesses (and devoureth their enemies). When this ministry goes into all the true churches, God's people will come into "the unity of the faith, and of the knowledge of the Son of God, unto a perfect man, unto the measure of the stature of the fullness of Christ." In this way if any understanding (man) tries to harm the ministry (hurt them), this false understanding will be killed by the fiery preaching coming from the witnesses (he must in this manner be killed).

Verse and Interpretation

Rev 11:5 And if any man will hurt them, fire proceedeth out of their mouth, and devoureth their enemies: and if any man will hurt them, he must in this manner be killed.

And if any false doctrine (man) tries to harm the ministry coming forth from the anointed ministers in the John the Baptist Company (them,) the fiery, anointed words (fire) coming out of their mouths (proceedeth) will destroy (devour) these false doctrines (their enemies). Any false belief (man) that tries to harm the ministry (hurt them) will be killed in this manner.

* * * * * * * * *

Rev 11:6 These have power to shut heaven, that it rain not in the days of their prophecy: and have power over waters to turn them to blood, and to smite the earth with all plagues, as often as they will.

No Rain

As I stated already, many of the miracles that took place literally in the Old Testament have a spiritual, not literal, counterpart in the New Testament. Elijah told Ahab it would not rain for three and a half years, and his words came to pass. I believe that in this New Testament account regarding the two witnesses, the withholding of rain has a spiritual rather than literal interpretation.

Rain in the Scriptures is usually a good thing. Rain brings blessings and abundant harvests. To shut up heaven is to take away blessings. When the witnesses are preaching the pure word of God, if those who hear the preaching decide they disagree or don't want to comply with what God is telling them, the Lord will permit some kind of calamity to come against them. God does this out of his great love for them. The John the Baptist Company of ministers won't afflict them. Their only responsibility will be to give the words of God to the people. God will not afflict the people but he will remove a portion of his protection long enough for some trouble to reach them. His sole purpose is that he might have a church with pure hearts devoid of any false doctrine.

Only when all false doctrines are removed will the church be able to come into the unity necessary to be the bride without spot or wrinkle that God desires for his Son. He knows that sometimes we need the extra impetus afforded by difficulties in order to move forward spiritually. It is quite possible that the difficulties people face will be tailor-made to their false beliefs. When they apply their false doctrines to no avail, they will be more willing to let go of these beliefs. This may take a long time for some people who have defended their erroneous doctrines over many years and even taught them. This will be difficult for them to admit and release. This will be humbling for them which will be a very good thing.

Waters Turned to Blood

Turning water to blood reminds us of Moses and the plagues God brought upon the Egyptian people to facilitate the release of the Hebrew slaves. Because of this, many people believe that one of the two witnesses is Moses. However, as we shall see again, that which was outwardly literal in the Old Testament has a more spiritual and eternal counterpart in the New Testament.

As we look to the Scriptures for our interpretation of this, two passages come to mind. The first is in Ephesians 5:

> Husbands love your wives even as Christ also loved the church, and gave himself for it; That he might sanctify and cleanse it with the washing of water by the word, That he might present it to himself a glorious church, not having spot, or wrinkle, or any such thing; but that it should be holy and without blemish (Eph 5:25-27).

This fits in perfectly with our interpretation of Revelation 11 as being God's preparation of his church to be the bride of Christ. Based on this, our interpretation for "water" will be the Word of God which is the Bible.

What about the blood? For this we turn to the Old Testament:

> Only be sure that thou eat not the blood: for the blood is the life; and thou mayest not eat the life with the flesh (Deu 12:23).

This and other passages in the Law reveal that the life is in the blood. Therefore, blood represents life.

Putting this together we can see that a good spiritual interpretation for having "power over the waters to turn them to blood" is that the witnesses' preaching will have the power to bring the Scriptures (water) to life (blood) for the people. This will help them mature and grow spiritually as they go through times of distress.

Smiting the Earth with Plagues

This brings us to the last power in this verse, the power to smite the earth with plagues. Are they striking the literal terrene globe or its inhabitants? I believe earth here refers to our physical bodies that God made out of dust (Gen 2:7) and are sometimes referred to as clay in the Scriptures.

It would make no sense to smite the earth itself as it is already enduring manmade plagues from which it may never recover aside from a great miracle of God. Nuclear radiation is only one example of this. The radiation released from the Fukushima nuclear power plant disaster of March 2011 has not ceased. The damaged reactors continue to pour radioactive plumes into the air and hundreds of tons of radioactive water into the Pacific Ocean daily. This radioactivity has spread to the Atlantic Ocean as well as all over the globe. Governments of the world are silent about this grave disaster of biblical proportions. This may exceed any disaster that has ever been. The earth could recover from the great flood, but the radioactivity from nuclear fission leaves behind dangerous components that remain poisonous to life for over a hundred thousand years.

Many nations possess nuclear weapons. Do we really think they won't eventually use them on each other… and us? The earth is already becoming uninhabitable in several places because of dangerous radioactive fallout… Chernobyl in Russia being one example of this.

The entire food supply of the earth is threatened because of genetic modification that has changed the molecular structure of some of our basic food crops to the point that they no longer produce seeds that can be replanted to produce a crop the following year. These are only two examples of numerous potential disasters of biblical proportions that are the possible fate of a world run amuck with sin.

Our weather is being geo-engineered to the extent that it is now controlled by men rather than by the natural means first determined by our Creator. The living organisms in our oceans are dying. Chemtrail spraying from airplanes deployed all over our planet are depositing heavy metals and health destroying particulates into the air that damage not only human health, but also all the animals and plants on the earth. The ozone layer itself is being destroyed. Mankind has played God and is destroying the entire planet (Wigington).

For the above reasons, I don't believe the witnesses will be inflicting plagues on our literal earth. Our earth is sick now in ways too numerous to recount, and a sick earth makes for sick inhabitants. The people listening to the witnesses will have conditions conducive to sickness all around them and should God withdraw his protective hand, they will succumb to them.

If the people listening to the preaching of the witnesses decide to reject their teaching, the Lord may withdraw his protective hand and allow them to experience physical distress in their body. Sometimes the only way we will change inwardly is if some outward affliction troubles us. As the Psalmist said:

Before I was afflicted I went astray: but now have I kept thy word (Psa 119:67).

It is good for me that I have been afflicted; that I might learn thy statutes (Psa 119:71).

I believe there may be some afflictions in their bodies that the Lord will use to motivate the people do whatever is necessary to come into perfection. I know in my own life there have been some spiritual issues I was not able to overcome until I experienced a physical affliction. I know the affliction was from the Lord because he warned me in a dream about it. Even with the warning I was not able to overcome until I suffered the physical affliction. After this experience I was able to appreciate more deeply the words of the above verses from Psalms. I just could not change my deeply engrained false belief of a lifetime that happened to be rooted in my identity until I suffered physical pain.

Now I would like to bring together all three parts of this verse into a succinct few sentences for a spiritual interpretation. This interpretation is to be understood contextually in light of the previous verse where it was seen that false doctrines and beliefs held by church people would oppose the deep truths being presented by the witnesses. According to the previous verse, these false understandings must be killed. This present verse reveals that some people will have to go through some difficult circumstances in their lives before they will be willing to let go of their wrong beliefs and receive the truth being preached by the witnesses.

Verse and Interpretation

Rev 11:6 These have power to shut heaven, that it rain not in the days of their prophecy: and have power over waters to turn them to blood, and to smite the earth with all plagues, as often as they will.

The John the Baptist Company of ministers filled with the Holy Spirit (These) will have the power to withhold blessings from the lives of persons who oppose their teaching in order that the people can go through difficult experiences that will reveal to them that their doctrine, when put to the test, is actually false (power to shut heaven that it rain not). At the same time they are experiencing these difficulties, the ministers, by their preaching, will be bringing the Scriptures (water) to life for them (blood). Those who oppose the teachings may also suffer physical afflictions until they are ready to discard their false doctrines and receive the truth as taught by the witnesses.

* * * * * * * * *

CHAPTER III

Rev 11:7 And when they shall have finished their testimony, the beast that ascendeth out of the bottomless pit shall make war against them, and shall overcome them, and kill them.

The beast can only make war against them at the time determined by God when they will have finished the assignment he has given them. They have gone into the churches. They have preached the word of God that has measured the hearts of the people. The people have separated as God has been judging his church. Now it is time for them to finish their testimony.

The Beast

This is the same beast as described in Revelation 13. I have explained the identity of this beast in my video series on Revelation 13 where I reveal this beast as being the law of sin. His head was wounded to death in Romans 7:8 where Paul said, "without the law sin was dead." And then in Romans 7:9 his deadly wound is healed, "When the commandment came, sin revived." We see then that sin was dead and then sin revived. Therefore, this beast is the law of sin.

As for its seven heads, numbers are always determined by their spiritual meaning in my interpretations. Seven means that he represents completeness of evil. Heads, *kephale* in Greek, is defined as being from the word *kapto*, (in the sense of seizing); the head (as the part most readily taken hold of). Putting this together we see that the law of sin has completely (seven) seized everything (heads).

The bottomless pit is inside of every person. It is the very source of the sin nature that all of us were born with. We can reckon ourselves dead to sin and alive unto God, but the pit is still deep inside us all. God will thoroughly deal with this and remove it in the end times. We will look at this in more detail towards the end of this book.

I don't believe the beast is going to literally kill the witnesses. For one thing, the Holy Spirit is part of the two witnesses and the Holy Spirit cannot be killed. The people are not going to be killed. They are a company of people representing the John the Baptist ministry. Their ministry is going to be killed.

This beast shall make war against their ministry and shall overcome it and kill it. Instead of this beast being some monster rising up out of the sea with seven heads, this is the law of sin that is in all people. Carnal people in churches acting out of the law of sin within them will come against the ministry and try to kill the ministry. It is the cross that slays the sin in us, but this teaching is sadly missing in many churches today. The only way to overcome carnality is to die to it. When Christians refuse to take up their cross daily they remain carnal and often persecute the ones who have chosen to die to self. When a ministry dies, God will resurrect it in greater power than it had before.

If you've ever spent much time in a church, you've learned that there are a lot of wars going on right inside the churches. There may be war between one church and another that differs in doctrine. There can be wars going on within the individual church amongst its members. There can be a lot of opposition in the very churches that were supposed to demonstrate God's love to the unbelievers.

"And they'll know we are Christians by our love..." so goes the words of a song we used to sing in church. Sometimes the opposition is over whether or not they think the minister is preaching the word of God. Eventually they may overcome these ministers and drive them out. So to kill them is to kill the ministry rather than the people themselves.

I've seen this happen numerous times when pastors go into churches full of faith and the Spirit of God, and they preach their hearts out to the people. The people in the church choose sides.

Those who oppose the minister build their army, so to speak, and come against him. They go to the overseers in the church structure and try to run him out. In this way they can eventually kill the ministry. The minister may move on to another church but very often the ministers who have been treated in this way just leave the ministry. I've seen this happen several times to people I know personally. They were very gifted and dedicated, but they just couldn't take all the hatred and the opposition that came forth against them right in their own churches.

We've been through it several times. It can be devastating, but looking back on it all we now understand that it was part of our preparation for ministry in the end times. Jesus said,

These things I command you, that ye love one another. If the world hate you, ye know that it hated me before it hated you (John 15:17, 18).

The surprise came in being hated in the churches. People in the world have been nice to us. What has happened is that the church has been infiltrated by carnal people and even Satanists who can be easily influenced by the enemy. They come against the minister and try to drive him out of the ministry.

Now I will bring this all together for my written interpretation of verse seven.

Verse and Interpretation

Rev 11:7 And when they shall have finished their testimony, the beast that ascendeth out of the bottomless pit shall make war against them, and shall overcome them, and kill them.

When the time comes determined by God that the witnesses have completed the task God assigned them, then the law of sin (beast) will rise up out of the carnal sin nature (bottomless pit) within some of the church people to oppose the ministry (war), drive the ministers out of the established church (overcome) and thereby kill the ministry.

* * * * * * * * *

Rev 11:8 And their dead bodies shall lie in the street of the great city, which spiritually is called Sodom and Egypt, where also our Lord was crucified.

Dead Bodies

First of all, let's identify what these dead bodies actually are. "Dead bodies" in the Greek is one word, *ptoma*. It also means "a downfall, a failure." There are six other Greek words that are translated "dead," but the particular word used here, *ptoma*, is the only one that means "a downfall or a failure." Of course, it also means "dead," but it does have these alternative definitions. I believe the dead bodies in this passage represent the ministry that has "died" or rather that has fallen down in seeming failure. The words "shall lie" are not in the Greek.

The words "great city" in the Bible are usually referring to Jerusalem and Jerusalem is a type of the church. The ministry is dead in the street of that city; however, it can be alive somewhere else. Now we need to discover more about this great city. The word "street" in the Greek is *plateia*, and it means "a wide place." Jesus taught us that wide is the gate and broad is the way that leads to death but narrow is the gate that leads unto life. We need to ask the question, Why would the church be a wide gate? That says something right there about the condition of the church. This downfall or seeming failure takes place in a church that is in a wide place. This kind of church wants the wide way, the broad way, the easy way. The churches that are willing to sacrifice everything for the Lord, that are willing to go the narrow way, the difficult way… they're the ones that would not see this ministry as being a failure. So the great city here is a type of Jerusalem which is a type of the church.

Sodom and Egypt

The rest of this verse will tell us more about this church. "Which is spiritually called Sodom and Egypt, where also our Lord was crucified." We all know the story of Sodom and Gomorrah. Sodom represents the kind of sin worthy of complete destruction. Egypt is a type of the world. Here we see that the church has become spiritually a place where there is so much sin it is absolutely worthy of destruction, and it has become just like the world.

Our last incontrovertible proof of this city's identity is seen here in the clause, "where also our Lord was crucified." It was the Lord's own people that had him crucified. It was the Jewish leaders, the ones that were thought of as being respectable and learned, who hated Jesus and plotted his death. These same kinds of people are ruling over many of our churches today. They persecute the true ministers and kill their ministries even as the religious leaders of Jesus' day had him crucified. It only takes a few carnal church people to complain to the religious leaders behind the back of the minister, and that ministry can be brought down almost overnight.

This may sound bleak, but we must remember that God is on his throne and ultimately his will and purpose will be achieved in his church. As we shall see in the ensuing verses, the supernatural power of God is going to come upon his faithful ministers, and they will be raised into a dimension of ministry more powerful than the world has ever seen. As Jesus said in John 14:12:

> *Verily, verily, I say unto you, He that believeth on me, the works that I do shall he do also; and greater works than these shall he do; because I go unto my Father. (John 14:12)*

We will see this take place on this earth very soon. The evil powers of our age are so massive and powerful that only through the supernatural power of God will anyone survive. The time is upon us where we need to seek first the kingdom of God and enter in as he is our only hope for the future. It is time for the kingdom to come on earth and for us to enter in. The book of Revelation will be showing us the way.

Verse and Interpretation

Rev 11:8 And their dead bodies shall lie in the street of the great city, which spiritually is called Sodom and Egypt, where also our Lord was crucified.

The ministry to prepare the way of the Lord (Their) seemed to be a failure (dead bodies) in the wide, broad way (street) of the church (the great city) that was spiritually corrupted by sin reminiscent of Sodom and by worldly influences (Egypt). The church leaders killed the present day ministry in the church similarly to the way the religious leaders killed Jesus in their attempts to stop his ministry (where also our Lord was crucified).

* * * * * * * * *

> Rev 11:9 And they of the people and kindreds and tongues and nations shall see their dead bodies three days and an half, and shall not suffer their dead bodies to be put in graves.

The first part of this verse, "and they of the people and kindreds and tongues and nations" reveals that what is going on in the churches is happening all over the world. It can be known by everyone because of the worldwide proliferation of the electronic media. Or even without the media…if you live in a small town and the church begins to struggle and half the people are against the minister and half want him to stay…it can become the talk of the whole town where everyone knows about it. Certainly what is going on in the churches does affect everyone in some way.

No Burial Permitted

It says here that everyone will see their dead bodies. A ministry doesn't exactly have a dead body but it can leave behind some remains of the ministry. Even though the ministry has been killed and perhaps the minister has left town, there may be left behind the books he has written or perhaps other literature he provided for the church members. Most churches record their services. Therefore many CDs of the ministry may still be in homes of the people or stacked in a corner of the church building. Perhaps they built a church building while they were there. There will be visible things left behind as a result of the ministry that was brought forth there. Additionally the deposit made in the hearts and the minds of the people will remain and can be seen in their changed lives.

This goes on for "three days and a half." We will interpret this according to the spiritual meaning of the numbers. Three is the number of completion. Half can mean "division or separation." Putting these together my interpretation is: This takes place for the period of time necessary (days) to bring completion (three) of separation (half) between the true believers who believed in the ministry and those who rejected it. What happens in the church even goes out into the town where people talk. People choose sides even when they weren't involved in the church. Some are for the ministry and some are against it. As people talk they are revealing what is in their hearts.

Our Testimony

I would like to share how this happened to my husband and me. In 1978 after pastoring for five years in a mainline denomination, we started an independent church in a small town of about 600 residents in the cornfields of Indiana. There were five churches in that little berg and ours was the "goingest" thing in town. This small town seemed like a great place to raise our two daughters, and we were very happy there. We had big plans for our little church, but a few months after our congregation formed, the Jim Jones massacre occurred in November of that year.

For those too young to remember, Jim Jones, pastor of a large church in California, led over a thousand of his members to a plot of land in Guyana where they were supposedly going to build a utopian community called "Jonestown." Things did not go well for them, and it wasn't long before many of the people realized they were virtual prisoners of Jim Jones surrounded by jungle with no way of escape. In the U.S., worried family members and friends of the duped congregation entreated congress to send a delegation to investigate. This congressional group, headed by Leo Ryan, wound up being shot to death near their plane in the jungle, and 913 members of the cult were murdered by their leaders when forced to drink cyanide-laced punch.

When this news broke in America, the gossip mongers in Indiana (and probably worldwide) lost no time in spreading the lie that any religious group not associated with a recognized denomination was a cult. Rumors quickly spread in our small town and in all the surrounding towns that my husband was another

Jim Jones. People believed that he forced everyone in our church to sign over their paychecks to him and made the women give him all their expensive jewelry. It was said that we sacrificed chickens on the altar of our church and that my husband threw Bibles on the ground and stomped on them.

When we would walk down the sidewalk in our little town, anyone approaching us would cross the street and continue down on the other side to avoid us. This little town had an old-fashioned drugstore with a soda fountain where townspeople would congregate with their friends over coffee and snacks. If one of us walked into the store, conversation would stop and people would stare at us. Youngsters would come up to our daughters in the local tri-county high school with comments such as, "I know who your dad is. He's that cult leader!"

Our house was on the main road in the center of the town. Our two daughters delivered the newspaper to the whole town—one girl had the south side and the other had the north. Sometimes one of us would walk the route with the girls just to have quality time with them. The point I want to make here is that we were visible. Everyone in that town could see how we lived and how our daughters behaved. We had lived in that community and been involved in its affairs for two years before we formed this little church. Not only that, my husband had recently graduated with his Master of Divinity degree from a reputable seminary in Indianapolis.

None of this mattered to the townspeople. Their minds had been taken over by powerful spiritual forces and nothing we said or did could change their minds. We were not able to win this battle regarding our reputation, but we won the battle for our own souls. We chose to forgive those who persecuted us and bless those who cursed us.

People's hearts were revealed. There was an elderly couple living next door to us who did not believe the lies. They had good hearts and did not succumb to the lies promulgated against us in the community. However, just two doors down from them was an elderly widow whose sidewalk my husband had for years freely shoveled when it snowed. She believed the lies. It was such a surprise to see how the sides split over us. We learned that only God sees the hearts of the people. People we believed were good friends turned against us. Others we hardly knew did not believe the lies. We were the issue that God used to deal with the hearts of the people.

Our ministry there did not die. It just moved "underground" into the homes of our faithful members. The seminary from which my husband graduated should have offered a course on how to endure persecution. We were totally unprepared and mystified by the whole experience. Now we are much older and wiser and God has been building in us the discerning of spirits to strengthen us and help us discern the hearts of those around us.

To finish this verse we need to examine the last clause, "and shall not suffer their dead bodies to be put in graves." From experience I can truly say that people don't easily drop the gossip regarding what they perceive happened in the church. They don't let it be buried so everyone can move on with their lives. They can keep it going for years.

Ten years after we moved away from that town to another state, friends of ours who had been in our church there and also moved away, decided to open a Subway franchise in a town about nine miles from the town where we were "crucified." They hired a young woman from our former town… someone we had never met. She had not been working there long when she asked the question, "Did you hear about the cult leader that used to live in our town who took the valuables of the people and made them sign over their paychecks to him?"

Our friends sat her down and began to reason with her. They pointed out to her that one of the church members who had believed in us was a state senator and also the principal of the local tri-county high school our children attended. They answered her question with a question of their own, "Do you really believe that _____, our state senator and high school principal, signed his paycheck over to Stoner Clark?" She thought for a minute and then saw the foolishness of what she had said. "No, of course not," was her answer. What a perfect example of not allowing the remains of the ministry to be buried.

Verse and Interpretation

Rev 11:9 And they of the people and kindreds and tongues and nations shall see their dead bodies three days and an half, and shall not suffer their dead bodies to be put in graves.

This upheaval in the established churches is going on all over the world. It can be known by everyone because of the worldwide electronic media and also because of the gossip of local people. The remains of the ministry (dead bodies) are visible…the books, CDs, videos, buildings, etc. and also the changed lives of the people. This continues for the period of time necessary to bring completion of separation (three days and a half) between the true believers who received the ministry and those who rejected it. When the churches separate because of this powerful ministry, those who opposed the ministry won't drop the issue but keep it ongoing with their gossip (bodies not put in graves).

* * * * * * * * *

Rev 11:10 And they that dwell upon the earth shall rejoice over them, and make merry, and shall send gifts one to another; because these two prophets tormented them that dwelt on the earth.

Rejoicing Over Their Deaths

Spiritually speaking, to dwell upon the earth can mean to live in a worldly manner focused on things of the earth rather than higher, more heavenly things. The people who rejoice over the demise of the ministry are carnal people who live spiritually in a lower realm. When you are the object of people's gossip you sometime wonder if those people really have a life or are they just so bored they don't have anything else to do but talk about others?

Sending gifts to one another happens when people become good friends. When there is an issue in a community that some people oppose, they often become friends with like-minded people with whom they would not normally fraternize. It is quite possible that they literally would give each other gifts.

As for tormenting people...certainly the godly prophets did not torment anybody. If the people felt tormented by them it was because their own conscience was hurting them.

There is something in the carnal nature of humankind that wants to believe bad things about other people. They like to talk about people and report bad things. They celebrate because they no longer have to listen to the convicting words that tormented their conscience. That is why they are rejoicing that the ministry is gone because it can no longer convict them of their own sin.

I've been talking about this happening on a small scale. I believe we are going to see it happen worldwide, and even now we can see the United States building up to this. In the mainstream media Christians are almost always made to look like fools in movies and television programs. If an alleged criminal ever had contact with a church, that is what they'll emphasize in their news reports...e.g. "this sixty year old Sunday School teacher held up a bank and escaped with everyone's hard-earned savings." You aren't told that he taught for about a month in some church thirty years ago before the Christians ran him out after discerning his true character.

Christians are going to become the scapegoats for everything evil that happens. In America in April of 2013 when the Boston Marathon bombings took place, the first news reports said they suspected right-wing extremists of the crime...right-wing extremists often being Christians and people who believe in the Constitution and the Bill of Rights. This hits the public over and over again...perhaps hundreds or thousands of times... until people begin to believe that Christians are the cause of everything wrong in our nation. (This is the same tactic Hitler used against the Jews.) Even though Christians are not ultimately the cause of the crime, all the media has to say is they are suspected. Eventually people start believing it even though it has never been proven true.

The public will rejoice when they are able to shut down the churches and they no longer have to be reminded of the gospel. Taking all references to Christ out of Christmas also soothes their consciences.

Verse and Interpretation

Rev 11:10 And they that dwell upon the earth shall rejoice over them, and make merry, and shall send gifts one to another; because these two prophets tormented them that dwelt on the earth.

The people who have chosen to live a worldly life of satisfying their own selfish lusts and who have joined with like-minded others to oppose this ministry (them that dwell on earth) rejoice (send gifts) because their conscience will no longer prick them now that the ministry is finished.

* * * * * * * * *

Rev 11:11 And after three days and an half the Spirit of life from God entered into them, and they stood upon their feet; and great fear fell upon them which saw them.

Just when the Devil thought he had won after Jesus was crucified, Jesus rose from the dead. There is a principle of death and resurrection that should be in every ministry that is truly of God. As long as the ministry is being done by us in our own power, God cannot do what he wants through the ministry. If we are willing to allow God to take that ministry down into death, he will raise it up in resurrection life. God does that with individuals; he does it with churches; and he is doing it with this particular move of God I call the John the Baptist ministry. It has gone down into death, but God had planned from its inception that it would die and then be resurrected in power at his appointed time.

Three and a Half days

Here we see the Spirit of God entering into this ministry after three days and a half. The Holy Spirit has been in it all along but this is a greater infilling of the Spirit of God. Three is the number of completion. Half is a number of division or separation. This is showing it was a period of time (days) that was necessary to complete (three) the judging of hearts so that believers could be separated from unbelievers (half). If you will remember back in the first verse of Revelation 11, the two witnesses were called to measure the temple. They did this by preaching a word that was measuring the hearts of the people.

When this ministry goes into the churches and the Word of God is preached, people have to decide if they are going to accept this ministry or reject it, and thereby God does a work of dividing. He has to divide and separate out from true believers those who just come to church for their own carnal reasons. Some may come because they see their friends there or it makes them look good in the eyes of the community. Perhaps they attend because it is what people do on certain holidays such as Christmas and Easter (C&E Christians). He has to separate those out from true believers who are sincerely following the Lord and who are willing to die to self and let Christ live through them. So there has been a mighty work going on to judge the hearts of the people. This has been a very necessary work and we see here that even though the ministry appears to have been silenced, it is only for a brief period of time.

Based on all the above I would interpret the first part of this verse as follows: When the time was completed (three) whereby everyone concerned had had the opportunity to choose for or against the ministry which was the same a choosing for or against God (half = division), the Spirit of life from God entered into the ministry.

Great Fear

This ministry that everyone thought was dead was merely going through a process deemed necessary by God to prepare the ministers to receive his great power. Before this it had been good ministry, but now, with this new infilling of God's Spirit, it becomes a very supernatural ministry. It will become apparent to anyone seeing this ministry that it is of God. Those who rejected and persecuted it will experience great fear because they will realize they rejected what was of God and now there are going to be consequences for this.

I believe the timeframe here corresponds to that of the ten virgins… five of whom were wise and five were foolish (Matt 25). The fact that they were virgins suggests that they all considered themselves to be Christians. However, when the Bridegroom came, those who had not prepared by keeping oil for their lamps were not able to enter into the marriage ceremony. They asked the wise virgins to share their oil, but they refused. Frankly, I don't think it is possible to share our oil. I can't give my faith or experience with God to anyone else. Each of us must find this for ourselves. I suspect that those who reject the John the Baptist ministry are likely to find themselves being counted as foolish virgins.

Verse and Interpretation

Rev 11:11 And after three days and an half the Spirit of life from God entered into them, and they stood upon their feet; and great fear fell upon them which saw them.

When the time was completed (three) whereby everyone concerned had had the opportunity to choose for or against the ministry which was the same as choosing for or against God (half – divided), the Spirit of life from God entered into the ministry. The ministry arose in power (stood on their feet) causing those who had rejected it to realize they had been wrong and that there would be consequences for this (fear fell).

* * * * * * * * *

Rev 11:12 And they heard a great voice from heaven saying unto them, Come up hither. And they ascended up to heaven in a cloud; and their enemies beheld them.

If we think heaven is somewhere up in the atmosphere and they were lifted up off the literal earth, then we're going to think God is deserting everybody else. I don't believe that is what this means, and as we look at this in a spiritual sense and examine what some of these words mean, we will see that God is calling them up to a higher spiritual dimension in him.

In a Cloud

The scripture says they ascended up to heaven in a cloud. What is a cloud? Is it those white fluffy collections of water vapor that we see floating in the sky? Or is it something spiritual? If we look at the word "cloud" all through the Bible, the cloud is often representative of the Spirit of God and the glory of God. Let's look at 2 Chronicles 5:

> It came even to pass, as the trumpeters and singers were as one, to make one sound to be heard in praising and thanking the LORD; and when they lifted up their voice with the trumpets and cymbals and instruments of music, and praised the LORD, saying, For he is good; for his mercy endureth for ever: that then the house was filled with a cloud, even the house of the LORD; So that the priests could not stand to minister by reason of the cloud: for the glory of the LORD had filled the house of God (2 Chron 5:13, 14).

It is not difficult to see the type here. We are the house of God individually and corporately. The cloud is the Spirit of God and the glory of God that is filling the ministers and the ministry and lifting them up into a higher dimension. It will be evident to all who see them that the presence and power of God have filled them. Even the persons who opposed them will see that this is so. The demons will also see and fear because of the Presence that fills them.

The Greek word for heaven is *ouranos* which can be defined as "elevation, the sky, the abode of God, the gospel, and air." There is a sense in which this word can be used to refer to the sky when we think of the stars in the heavens, but for our understanding here, I believe "the abode of God" is the best definition. When Almighty God fully indwells us, seen in type here as the cloud filling the temple, then we are in heaven even if we are still in a physical body on earth. When we die to self and the Spirit of God fills our whole being as the cloud filled the temple, then we will be in a realm similar to the one Jesus was in when he walked among us performing miracles and teaching.

In my interpretation of Revelation, I see the previous chapters, when viewed inwardly, as depicting a progressive process believers will go through in the end times to come into spiritual perfection. When the two witnesses begin their ministry, the John the Baptist Company has gone through this process as revealed in the earlier chapters. They have gone through their own death to self and resurrection before beginning this ministry. In Revelation 11, the ministry itself goes down into death and then rises in perfection, and the power of God is released through it. Once a ministry and those involved in the ministry have gone down into death and been raised in resurrection life, God can pour his power through it because these people will not be corrupted by power. Their character will be humble and they will be so one with Christ that they will only do what the Father says.

God is not going to forsake everyone. He is going to have a powerful ministry that will be ministering to the needs of the people in the world. The judgment of God will be evident in the world but God's judgment is always redemptive in nature. It is God's will that all would repent of their sins and turn to him. This ministry will go forth; others will be brought to the Lord who will in turn go down into death and resurrection. Then God will also say to them, "Come up hither" and they too will go forth and minister. In this way the gospel will quickly and exponentially spread throughout the entire world.

Verse and Interpretation

Rev 11:12 And they heard a great voice from heaven saying unto them, Come up hither. And they ascended up to heaven in a cloud; and their enemies beheld them.

And God called them up to a high spiritual realm (come up hither) where he dwells (heaven) and the presence and glory of God came upon them (cloud). This was observed by all who had opposed them including the demonic realm (enemies).

* * * * * * * * *

CHAPTER IV

> Rev. 11:13 And the same hour was there a great earthquake, and the tenth part of the city fell, and in the earthquake were slain of men seven thousand: and the remnant were affrighted, and gave glory to the God of heaven.

A Great Earthquake

At the same time that the witnesses ascend up to a higher realm in God and the presence and glory of God comes upon them, there is going to be a worldwide disaster of some sort as typified by the great earthquake. It could be the fall of the world's economies. One distinct possibility would be nuclear war and/or a nuclear disaster. As of this writing, radioactive plumes from the Fukushima nuclear plant disaster in Japan are continuing to rise up into the atmosphere and tons of radioactive water are pouring into the Pacific Ocean polluting Hawaii, Alaska, and the United States mainland as well as other places with deadly radioactive fallout. This is not reported in our mainstream media, but numerous alternative news sites are reporting this and backing up their claims with solid, scientific evidence. Then there is the whole disaster of the world's food supply being endangered by genetic engineering, the massive die-off of our honeybees and the overuse of pesticides among other things. Whatever this Revelation 11 disaster is, it will be of such a great magnitude that multitudes will be in great fear.

We need to remember that whatever earthshaking disaster occurs, this great ministry will be ready to bring God, first of all to the faithful in the church, and then to the world. God will be ministering to the lost and the frightened people who are open to him.

Also at the time of the great earthquake we are told that a "tenth part of the city fell." I already established early in this teaching that the city is Jerusalem, and Jerusalem is a type of the church. As always we don't want to view numbers for their numerical value but for their spiritual meaning. Ten is the number of perfection of divine order. The tenth part would mean all that falls short of the perfection of divine order. This disaster will cause all in the church that falls short of the perfection of divine order to fall.

The church as we know it today is not in the perfection of divine order. It is still dominated by the effects of the Dark Ages and particularly the edicts of the emperor Constantine who considered himself to be a Christian. He commanded that church buildings be constructed and gave special favors to the pastors. Once the church stopped meeting in homes the world came into the church. With the advent of favored professional ministers, the priesthood of all believers ceased and the church lost its vibrant life and power. It is necessary for God's purposes that this be brought down. Out of the ashes God will build the church his way, and his two witnesses will have a major part in facilitating this.

This leads us to the next clause of this verse, "and in the earthquake were slain of men seven thousand." Men, according to the early Church Fathers, can represent understandings. Therefore, when this great disaster happens, a lot of understandings (men) that people have been holding onto and believing in will be revealed to be false. These false beliefs (men) will die as a result of this disaster.

There are seven thousand understandings (men) that die. The spiritual meaning of seven thousand would be the same as "seven" only intensified by the zeros. Seven means "spiritual completion." Therefore this is saying that what people believed to be spiritually complete understandings (men) died as a result of this great disaster. Not only will these understandings pass away, but the church leaders who taught these things will also be brought down. There are entire ministries that have gone out all over the world that are based in false doctrines. These will all crumble and die.

One major church doctrine comes to my mind that I know will fall when this disaster strikes, and that is the belief in the Rapture of the church. The concept that Christians don't have to go through suffering is quite foreign to the church of past ages that experienced being thrown to the lions, burned at the stake and many other extreme persecutions. All these people believed they were living in the last days and that the second coming of Christ was imminent. The Rapture doctrine is also not believed in many nations today where Christians are suffering for their faith. We don't hear much about suffering here in America, but many Christians around the world are imprisoned, tortured and killed for their faith even today. We find nothing about the Rapture in the writings of the early Church Fathers or any of the great Christian writers down through the centuries. The fact is the Rapture doctrine did not even exist before 1830 when a woman by the name of Margaret Macdonald had a vision of Christ returning twice… the first time to take away his church.

There will not be a sudden disappearance from the earth of all the godly people. However, there will be a lifting up of true believers that will be a spiritual lifting up such as represented in the previous verse where God says, "Come up hither." God wants to raise us up *spiritually* into a dimension of Spirit reserved for the church of the end times. When this great disaster strikes, a lot of erroneous things Christians have believed will come crashing down.

The last part of this verse states, "and the remnant were affrighted, and gave glory to the God of heaven." The remnant represents the people who received the ministry of the two witnesses and did not oppose them. Even these faithful ones will be frightened over this disastrous event, but they will still give glory to God. They will understand that God has a purpose in what has happened. One typical worldly response to a disaster is to curse God, but the faithful ones in the remnant will choose to worship God in spite of what has happened.

Verse and Interpretation

Rev 11:13 And the same hour was there a great earthquake, and the tenth part of the city fell, and in the earth-

quake were slain of men seven thousand: and the remnant were affrighted, and gave glory to the God of heaven.

At the same time as the witnesses ascend up to a higher realm in God and the glory of God comes on them (same hour), a worldwide disaster will strike (earthquake). This disaster will cause all in the church that falls short of the perfection of divine order (tenth part of the city) to fall. What people think are spiritually perfect understandings (seven thousand men) will die – trusted doctrines and ministries based in false beliefs will all fall. The people in the church who have not opposed the John the Baptist Company (remnant) will be frightened, and yet they will still give glory to God in heaven.

* * * * * * * * *

Rev 11:14 The second woe is past; and, behold, the third woe cometh quickly.

The Woes

There are three woes in Revelation. The word "woe" in the Greek means simply "an exclamation of grief." This does not mean it is necessarily a bad thing. It all depends on our relationship with Christ. The Bible says it is through much tribulation that we enter the kingdom of God (Acts 14:22). In times of tribulation we search our hearts before God, discard our idols, die to self, cling to Christ and are conformed more to his image.

The great shaking described in preceding verses is certainly woeful if you are trusting in idols. However, if you are seeking God with your whole heart and desiring his will be done on earth, then the shaking is good. It is necessary in order for God's kingdom to come on earth. God will not transpose his kingdom over the kingdoms the Devil has built up in the earth. These have to be torn down first. God's church cannot come into the perfection of divine order with truth and purity of heart until there is first a tearing down of all in the church that is not of God.

The church in its present condition cannot enter the kingdom of God. It is deeply divided over doctrine and practice. Once it is torn down, God can then build it up to contain the power and beauty he wants to display before the world. What a surprise that will be in the eyes of the world after witnessing the fall of church leaders in disgrace and scandal and seeing the weakness of a divided church. I am reminded of God's words to Jeremiah:

> Then the LORD put forth his hand, and touched my mouth. And the LORD said unto me, Behold, I have put my words in thy mouth. See, I have this day set thee over the nations and over the kingdoms, to root out, and to pull down, and to destroy, and to throw down, to build, and to plant (Jer 1:9, 10).

This is the second woe. The first woe was in Revelation nine where, in my interpretation, the challenge of the locusts, viewed spiritually as demons, revealed one part of a person's spiritual preparation necessary to be in the John the Baptist Company.

The third woe is in Revelation twelve where the Devil and his angels are cast down out of heaven onto the earth. This will mean great grief to those who are living a worldly life, but to those God is preparing, it will mean they have taken territory away from the Devil. They will have God's protection and great power.

Verse and Interpretation

> Rev 11:14 The second woe is past; and, behold, the third woe cometh quickly.

The ministry of judging the church is past (second woe), and very soon the Devil will be cast out of the heavenly realm onto the earth and cause great grief to all the inhabitants of the earth and sea (third woe).

* * * * * * * * *

> Rev 11:15 And the seventh angel sounded; and there were great voices in heaven, saying, The kingdoms of this world are become the kingdoms of our Lord, and of his Christ; and he shall reign for ever and ever.

The Seventh Angel Sounds

In both the Hebrew and Greek languages of the Bible angels are defined as being messengers. There is an important message coming from God through his messenger that has to do with the number "seven." Seven is the number of spiritual perfection. Therefore, this message is saying it is time for God's people to come into spiritual perfection. The messages that will be proclaimed are going to be specifically designed to help the church become the pure, spotless bride for whom the Bridegroom is coming.

There were great voices in heaven speaking forth these messages. Whose voices would these be? The fact that the two witnesses have ascended to heaven causes me to believe it is their voices that are being heard. Remember they are still on earth in physical bodies but they have been raised up by God into a very high spiritual realm in the presence of God called heaven. Their preaching is now even more powerful than before.

This is the reason the "third woe cometh quickly." Their powerful preaching will call the church upward to take her rightful place in heaven with them which will result in the Devil being cast down onto the earth. We see the church in Revelation 12 depicted as the woman who is "a great wonder in heaven." She is in this position because of her response to the preaching of the two witnesses.

The message the witnesses are preaching is a proclamation that it is time for the kingdom of God to come on earth. They are calling the church to come up to her rightful place of spiritual perfection so they can accomplish this mandate from God. Christians down through the ages have been praying, "Thy kingdom come, thy will be done on earth as it is in heaven." This is God's will. Jesus told us to pray this way and countless multitudes of Christians have prayed this prayer for the past 2000 years.

We see in this verse that God sees it as a fact. "The kingdoms of this world are become the kingdoms of our Lord and of his Christ." We just have to walk it out. We know that if we pray anything according to his will, he hears us and will give us that for which we have asked. There is no doubt this will be done. This will be accomplished as the powerful ministry of the John the Baptist Company and the Holy Spirit goes forth in great power to raise the church up into her rightful place in the heavenlies.

This will shock the world. However, this will not come to pass before the church is judged. There will be a great judgment upon the church, especially the church in America because we have been given more light than any other people who lived before us. Jesus warns us in his Word:

And that servant, which knew his lord's will, and prepared not himself, neither did according to his will, shall be beaten with many stripes, (Luke 12:47).

In spite of all our opportunities, we have become weak, divided and a laughing stock to the world. Many of us have been embarrassed to speak of Jesus. We have participated in the sins of our debauched society rather than standing against them and being the salt and light Jesus called us to be.

It used to be that no sporting event or community-wide program would be conducted on Sunday mornings because the Christians would all be in church. It has been sad to see this societal respect pass away because Christians have willingly chosen to participate in worldly activities on Sunday mornings rather than honor God with worship on that traditional day.

Church, for many, has become an activity to participate in if there is nothing else going on. There is just as much divorce, immorality and sin of all kinds in the church as in the world. Jesus is not pleased. If we think we will not be severely judged because we are Americans, we are in for a rude awakening. The Lord has shown us in his Word and also our particular church has had specific words from him that the judgment on the lukewarm Christians in America will exceed anything the world has ever seen.

Even though the majority of Christians have succumbed to the temptations of the world, God, as always, has had a remnant that has remained true to him. Through these people, he will reach the lost and establish his kingdom on earth. It may look impossible, but God likes to do the impossible because then all the glory will be given to him and no flesh will glory in his sight.

Verse and Interpretation

Rev 11:15 And the seventh angel sounded; and there were great voices in heaven, saying, The kingdoms of this world are become the kingdoms of our Lord, and of his Christ; and he shall reign for ever and ever.

A message comes forth (angel sounded) that it is time for people to come into spiritual perfection (seventh). This is coming from the ministers whose ministry died and was resurrected (voices in heaven). They are calling the remnant of the church that was judged to come into perfection that the kingdom of God can come on the earth as it is in heaven.

* * * * * * * * *

Rev 11:16 And the four and twenty elders, which sat before God on their seats, fell upon their faces, and worshipped God,

The Twenty-Four Elders

We have seen outwardly the ministry of the two witnesses, people's response to their message, the witnesses lifted up into heaven and their call to preach the kingdom of God coming on earth. Now in this verse, we will see what is taking place inwardly within the ministers.

In order to unlock this verse we need to use three keys:

- Inward not outward view
- Allegory
- Numbers have spiritual meaning only

As we view this verse inwardly it would be good to look at what Jesus said in Luke 17:

And when he was demanded of the Pharisees, when the kingdom of God should come, he answered them and said, The kingdom of God cometh not with observation:

Neither shall they say, Lo here! or, lo there! for, behold, the kingdom of God is within you (Luke 17:20, 21).

If the kingdom of God is to come on earth, it must first come in the hearts of the people. This is where we will find the four and twenty elders. They are within us and they have something to do with the way God created us and the work God has been doing in our lives. The twenty-four elders are in heaven. The twenty-four elders are within us because that heavenly realm is within us.

Our allegorical key comes from some of the great Christian teachers of the 3rd through 6th Centuries. According to these early Church Fathers (men like Ambrose, St. Augustine, and Gregory the Great), the word "men" can represent certain minds (Jukes, 63). Therefore, an elder, being a man, can represent a certain mind. As we interpret spiritually the meaning of the number "twenty-four," we will see exactly what kind of mind this is.

Twenty-four is the number of divine governmental perfection. Twelve is the number of governmental perfection on earth as seen in the twelve tribes of Israel. Twenty-four is the number of divine governmental perfection in heaven, the pattern of which can be seen in the twenty-four courses of the priestly service in the temple. If a mind is in divine governmental perfection (twenty-four), then this is a spiritual mind. The spiritual mind is in complete submission to the will of God. (Remember, we are not interpreting twenty-four for its numerical value but *only* for its spiritual meaning; therefore, within the person is one spiritual mind, not twenty-four.)

Sitting before God

Another indication as to the identity of the twenty-four elders is that they are seated in heaven. In Ephesians 2:6 we read that God "…hath raised us up together, and made us sit together in heavenly places in Christ Jesus." This verse is speaking about the position of our spirit. In our spirit we are seated in heavenly places with Christ Jesus even while our physical body is still living on earth.

The position of sitting implies "rest." Therefore, this is a mature spirit. This is a spirit that has entered into the rest of God as the Holy Spirit urges us to do in Hebrews:

> *There remaineth therefore a rest to the people of God. For he that is entered into his rest, he also hath ceased from*

his own works, as God did from his. Let us labour therefore to enter into that rest, lest any man fall after the same example of unbelief (Heb 4:9-11).

Putting this all together, we see in this verse an inward view of what it will be like spiritually in God's fully matured believers in the end times when "the kingdoms of this world are become the kingdoms of our Lord, and of his Christ; and he shall reign for ever and ever."

First the kingdom comes in the spirit of individual believers so that each believer is totally aligned with the will of God. When all believers come to this position, there will be total unity. They will be like the great army of the Lord described in the book of Joel:

They shall run like mighty men; they shall climb the wall like men of war; and they shall march every one on his ways, and they shall not break their ranks: Neither shall one thrust another; they shall walk every one in his path: and when they fall upon the sword, they shall not be wounded. They shall run to and fro in the city; they shall run upon the wall, they shall climb up upon the houses; they shall enter in at the windows like a thief. The earth shall quake before them; the heavens shall tremble: the sun and the moon shall be dark, and the stars shall withdraw their shining: And the LORD shall utter his voice before his army: for his camp is very great: for he is strong that executeth his word: for the day of the LORD is great and very terrible; and who can abide it? (Joel 2:7-11).

Here in Revelation we are shown a picture of a spirit that has come fully into the rest of God. This is the rest that the book of Hebrews encourages us to enter.

And to whom sware he that they should not enter into his rest, but to them that believed not? So we see that they could not enter in because of unbelief. Let us therefore fear, lest, a promise being left us of entering into his rest, any of you should seem to come short of it (Heb 3:18-4:1).

The Spiritual Mind Worships

Now that we understand that the twenty-four elders represent our spiritual mind that has come into the rest of God, we can continue with the rest of this verse that reveals more about our spiritual mind.

They (It) "…fell upon their faces, and worshipped God." The spiritual mind worships God continuously. This will be the activity of our spirit when we reach full maturity. It will be at rest and free to focus all its attention on God. It is seated with God and therefore is in God's presence.

One cannot help but worship God when one is in his presence. The love that emanates from him, his inimitable gentleness and sweetness is so magnificent all we want to do is worship. The more we worship him, the stronger we feel his glorious presence. This is truly the greatest joy and fulfillment any human being could ever imagine, but it only comes when our labors have ceased and we enter into his rest. Until this rest comes, we are incapable of experiencing what the spirit is feeling here. We may have experienced occasionally some semblance of this in some special circumstance, but not in this depth… and this is continual. The spiritual mind does not come and go from God's presence it remains there. At this level of maturity we are able to feel this glorious sense of God's presence and the feeling never leaves.

Verse and Interpretation

Rev 11:16 And the four and twenty elders, which sat before God on their seats, fell upon their faces, and worshipped God,

And their spiritual minds in governmental perfection (24 elders) which had come into rest (sat) and abode in the presence of God (before God) were continuously worshiping God and enjoying his presence.

* * * * * * * * *

CHAPTER V

> *Rev 11:17 Saying, We give thee thanks, O Lord God Almighty, which art, and wast, and art to come; because thou hast taken to thee thy great power, and hast reigned.*

In this verse we see why the ministers are at rest and able to continuously worship God. Some of the details about entering the rest of God are revealed in the words "which art, and wast, and art to come."

When we come into the rest of God, we have become reconciled to everything in our life in the present (which art), the past (and wast) and thereby we are able to also trust God completely for our future (and art to come).

Which Art

In order to enter into the rest of God, we have to be able to trust him completely for whatever challenges we are currently facing. When trials and difficulties come our way, if we are to be victorious, we have to find God in the midst of each trial. Every adverse event needs to be seen in the context of the metanarrative of God. We must back off from our myopic view of life and see it in the perspective of God's ultimate plan and purpose for our life.

Many years ago we were pastoring a church that grew rapidly and looked successful in the eyes of our denominational overseers and also to the community at large. Then, for no reason known to us, people began to leave the church. We went from needing to go to two services in order to accommodate the crowds to about twenty people.

My husband and I were greatly distressed over this situation. One day I was working at my kitchen sink thinking about the situation when I heard God's still small voice saying, "I didn't bring you here to build a big church. I brought you here to build you." I knew at that point that this had been a trial that was to prepare us for future ministry.

It was not long after that that we were transferred to a church in Western New York where we learned, in the course of time, that God had things for us there that we could not have entered into had we remained in the old church. God had to allow the church to dwindle in order to do a work in us and also to prepare us to move. I always wanted to put down roots but it had been God's purpose in each church we served to move us to another place. Each geographical move proved to also be a spiritual move upward.

Over the years we learned that whatever adversity we faced was permitted by God for his purpose, and if God permitted it, it was for our good because he has only good in his plans for us. In light of this, we learned to ask three questions: Where is God in this situation? What is he doing? And how am I responding? Over time we have learned to face the present in the rest of God knowing that he is in control and if we prayerfully look we will find his purpose in the midst of the difficulty.

One more question we have asked in the midst of adversity is, "Is God who he says he is?" When one is facing difficulties and serving God to one's best ability and yet it seems that every blessing is withheld, it becomes a challenge to believe God's Word is true. We continually answered this question by believing that God's Word is true, he is who he says he is, and he will bring good out of every situation. It is easy to love God when everything is going well and God's blessings are evident. It is another thing to love and serve God when all one can see is adversity, but this is what blesses God. We learned that first of all we needed to give God what he wanted and then trust him that at some point there would eventually be blessings for us.

Which Wast

Time does not heal all wounds. Everything in the past and present must be worked through in the presence of the Holy Spirit. There are many painful and disappointing things that have happened to us in life, some not of our doing, but also some resulting from decisions we have made, that in our fallen nature, we have blamed on God.

All these things must be brought before the Lord and dealt with completely.

When things happen in life, we form beliefs that are often inaccurate. We need to identify the lies we believed about ourselves and God in the midst of the circumstance. We need to repent of believing these lies and replace them with truth based on God's Word as revealed in the Bible. We need to forgive others for hurting us. We may need to forgive ourselves for making bad decisions. Additionally, in the midst of our disappointing circumstances we may have formed bitter root judgments that became self-imposed curses and affected our lives from that point forward. These judgments must be identified and renounced to break their effects over our lives. I would like to briefly give an example from my own life of a bitter root judgment that became a self-inflicted curse.

It seemed to me that I worked hard and did my best in all endeavors of my life, but I continually missed out on the blessings that should have been the result of my efforts. I was aware of the concept of bitter root judgments and knew I had one in my life, but for some reason I could not find the root of this judgment. It may be that I lacked the faith to believe that I could hear from God about this. After years of experiencing the painful results of having this judgment, there came a time when it happened again and this time when I prayed, I was able to hear God

As I got down on my knees and prayed for God to reveal this judgment to me, he showed me that when I was a four-year-old child I was upset that I never had a grandmother. It seemed to me that all my friends had grandmothers but both of mine died before I was born. I blamed God that he withheld from me the grandmothers that should have rightfully been mine. When I had this revelation, I cried and sobbed like a young child longing for a grandmother. I was able to ask God's forgiveness for judging him in this matter and the bitter root judgment was finally broken. I never again reaped that judgment in life. God opened doors before me and blessed me in many ways that had not been possible until I repented of my judgment against him.

In addition to bitter root judgments of which we are unaware, we have probably also made inner vows. My mother was a wonderful, godly woman who was outgoing and friendly. Her boldness sometimes embarrassed me, and unknown to me until God revealed it, I made the vow that I would never be bold like my mother. This locked me up into painful timidity that was only overcome when God revealed this vow to me in answer to my prayer. Breaking this vow had a tremendous effect on my life.

Bitter root judgments and inner vows are responses we have made unconsciously yet they are nevertheless binding on our lives. In fact, they profoundly affect our lives, but their power is easily broken once the judgment or vow is revealed to us, and we repent and break its hold over our life.

The point I want to make here is that all of us have many things from our past that cloud our concept of who God is and who we are in him. These all need to be cleared up before we can enter into the rest of God. It takes time and a diligent pursuit of God for these issues to be resolved.

Once we have thoroughly dealt with our past, we are able to look back and see that God was there. We can praise him for everything that happened because, in him, it has all worked together for good... both his and ours. We have come into rest in regards to our past.

It is an amazing thing that when we are thoroughly clear in our heart regarding our past, the present gets much better. Many adversities in our lives come because of sin in our heart that attracts the particular adversity we are encountering. When difficult situations arise, it is good to ask God what is inside us that he wants to show us. There is often a correlation.

And Art to Come

Once persons are reconciled with God regarding every issue in the past and are trusting God for the present, it is much easier to trust God with our future. As we have wrestled through all our past sins and concerns and seen God at work in our present, we have come to a new understanding of who we are in Christ. Having an identity based in our relationship with Jesus frees us of worry about the future.

It is easy to read that God is love, but knowing ourselves loved by him can only be understood as we clear our hearts of all the lies we have believed about God and ourselves... lies that were built up over years of making poor responses to life's challenges.

Our God Reigns

Now that we have examined the middle of this verse, we can include the first and last portions of the verse for a total picture of what the spiritual mind is doing at this point.

> *Rev 11:17 Saying, We give thee thanks, O Lord God Almighty, which art, and wast, and art to come; because thou hast taken to thee thy great power, and hast reigned.*

The spiritual mind is able to thank God for every aspect of this person's life... past, present and future... because this person sees that the power of God and the sovereignty of God have been present in their entire life. All the difficult situations have worked out for good by the power of God. No matter how terrible our experiences were at the time, we see that God had his way in them to bring us to where we are in him today. God has reigned. This mature, spiritual mind knows that without all the adversity it had to endure, it would have never come into this depth of relationship with Christ Jesus.

This is oil in the lamp! We cannot give this to anyone else. When Christ returns, there will be many Christians in outer darkness gnashing their teeth because they did not avail themselves of the opportunities provided them in life to come into the position of maturity seen here in the witnesses. It is easy for us Christians to assume that those in outer darkness weeping and gnashing their teeth will be unbelievers; however, the Scriptures indicate otherwise:

> *But the children of the kingdom shall be cast out into outer darkness: there shall be weeping and gnashing of teeth (Mat 8:12).*

We can stand in church and sing songs of praise about God's power and reign over all the earth, but until we have experienced and acknowledged this in our own lives, we won't truly understand what we are singing and our worship will lack the depth it could have.

Verse and Interpretation

> *Rev 11:17 Saying, We give thee thanks, O Lord God Almighty, which art, and wast, and art to come; because thou hast taken to thee thy great power, and hast reigned*

The witnesses in their spiritual minds were able to thank God for all things because they recognized his Almightiness manifested in all of life (Almighty God) including the present (which art), the past (and wast) and the future (art to come). They could see that God's power had worked all things together for good and his sovereign will had been accomplished in every aspect of their lives (hast reigned).

* * * * * * * * *

> *Rev 11:18 And the nations were angry, and thy wrath is come, and the time of the dead, that they should be judged, and that thou shouldest give reward unto thy servants the prophets, and to the saints, and them that fear thy name, small and great; and shouldest destroy them which destroy the earth.*

The Angry Nations

What happens or does not happen in the church affects the world, but few have the spiritual discernment to recognize this. It is easy for Christians in America to see the terrible mess our nation is in and blame it on our ungodly leaders. However, if we had obeyed and served Jesus, our light would have shone brightly enough to quell much of the great darkness now descending upon us and the world. Instead of influencing our society for good, we have allowed ourselves to be influenced by our society for evil.

Here in this verse we see the reaction of the world to the witnesses' high place in God. They are angry. You won't hear this announced in the news, but what happens in the spiritual realm determines what happens in the natural. The demons know where the witnesses are spiritually and they don't want them influencing others. They are angry and their wrath is felt by the people of the world. Even though people may suffer because of the decisions made by national leaders who are influenced by the evil supernatural, God will use these misguided politicians to carry out his punishment on the world and even on wayward Christians.

The Old Testament is full of accounts where God's people participated in idolatry and refused to forsake it and turn back to the true and living God even though he pleaded with them through his prophets. God warned them of the terrible consequences of turning away from him but they did it anyway. Time and again, God permitted evil nations to come against his people, steal their land and take them captive as slaves to foreign lands… all because of their idolatry.

Why would it be any different today? God does not change. He still wants his people to love him and forsake their idols in order to have a relationship with him. If we don't turn to him he will again use heathen leaders and nations to discipline his people until we repent and turn back to him.

I truly believe the judgment of God that will fall on lukewarm Christians will be far worse than what the Israelites experienced through the Assyrians, Babylonians and others that conquered them. It will be worse because we have had more revelation, blessings and opportunities to know and follow God than any people who have ever lived on the face of the earth. Jesus warned us in Luke 12,

> And that servant, which knew his lord's will, and prepared not himself, neither did according to his will, shall be beaten with many stripes. But he that knew not, and did

commit things worthy of stripes, shall be beaten with few stripes. For unto whomsoever much is given, of him shall be much required: and to whom men have committed much, of him they will ask the more (Lu 12:47-48).

Maybe the greatest reason the church deserves harsher condemnation is that we have the incarnational reality of the New Covenant palpably demonstrated by the infilling of the Holy Spirit. Unlike Israel of old who only had outward manifestations of God, we have been privileged with his indwelling presence.

For us to put God at the bottom of our priority list and spend our time pursuing sports, recreation, careers, family and whatever else we worship is a slap in his face. Judgment will be worse also because the technology available to torture and kill people is far beyond anything the heathen nations of the Bible could have imagined. This is the time of the harvest when we will see the fullness of good and the fullness of evil. The fullness of evil will be directed at those the Devil hates the most... Christians. Yet, if we are willing to forsake all to follow Christ, I believe we will have his protection.

As Revelation 12 will reveal, the ministry of the two witnesses will cause a powerful church to emerge out of God's judgment and people will go forth in the fullness of Christ with power to minister to a lost and dying world. Those who made no time for God will be weeping and gnashing their teeth when they see what they could have had if they had only been faithful to their loving Savior. The faithful will rise up into the high place in God reserved for the church of the end times. It will be glory beyond anything we can imagine.

Let's examine the word "nations." This word in the Greek is *ethnos* from which we derive our word "ethnic." It is also defined as "people of the same habit." It can be interpreted as not only nations, but also ethnic groups, groups of like-minded people and in the spirit world it can be demons. Every day events take place worldwide that are reported in the news for the express purpose of causing strife and division amongst various people groups... blacks against whites, young against old, heterosexuals against homosexuals, poor against rich... and so it goes. Those in charge of the media want to cause division in hopes of stirring up riots such that martial law can be instituted and all freedoms gone.

The Judgment of the Dead

Some people interpret this to mean those who have died in the past are being judged. For the context of my particular interpretation, I see this as those alive on earth at this time who are dead spiritually and are being judged. I believe this judging has been transpiring for many years. Lines have been drawn repeatedly, people have taken sides and God has been watching. As the frightening events of the last of the last days descend upon us, all the decisions made up until this time will determine where each person lines up spiritually. Many will die in their sins. Others will recognize this as the great end time judgment of God and come to repentance.

Judgment Comes Before Rewards

Before we can receive any rewards from God, we must first pass through judgment. This is not to say everyone will stand before a big throne and listen for their name to be called to see whether or not they made it into heaven. The judgment I'm speaking of should be going on in our daily lives. Believers who have a relationship with God should have been aware of being in a process of judgment for many years... I know I have.

At first it was the big things that were judged--obvious idols and sinful thoughts that had to come down. God put his finger on anything I loved more than him... like husband and children. God arranged circumstances where I had to make decisions and by making the right decisions, these idols came down in my heart and God was elevated to first place. I still love my family and have a terrific relationship with them, but God did a work in my heart, and I knew I had been judged. In more recent years the judging has become much more refined with every carnal thought, attitude and fleshly appetite having to die.

To give more clarity to this important concept, I would like to share how I died to my husband, Stoner, in a way that I still loved him dearly. It was a circumstance that God arranged... of this I have no doubt. It was in the early 1980s. We had very little income and in order to make ends meet, Stoner started driving a truck making deliveries for a new, local company that shipped women's clothing to stores in some Midwest and southern states. Although he only drove for this company for a few months, it turned out to be a trying experience partly due to the poorly maintained equipment they used. For example, failure to maintain the brakes on the trailers they used I felt put the drivers' lives in jeopardy.

The rig he drove was a pickup truck with a fifth wheel trailer attached. The brakes on the trailer did not work but the men who owned the company, men we knew personally, refused to do anything about it.

There was a time in the spring when Stoner was going to make a delivery to Atlanta, Georgia and I thought it would be nice to go along with him. It was still cold in Indiana and I wanted to feel the warmth of the South and see all the flowers that were undoubtedly blooming there. Besides, it would be nice to have this time together with my husband.

It was a terrible experience. To begin with, it was a very long drive. Traffic was heavy and fast. Drivers were reckless, and I kept thinking about the fact that there were no brakes on the trailer we were pulling. Once we got to Atlanta and made the delivery, we had great difficulty finding a motel that had a vacancy. Finally, in the wee hours of the morning, we found a place and got a few hours sleep before heading back to Indiana.

When we arrived home late that night, we fell into bed exhausted. After only four hours' sleep the phone rang. The truck company wanted him to make the same run again… right then.

I begged him not to go. I knew he was exhausted. I couldn't go again because I had to be home with our children (they had stayed with friends for our trip). How could he stay awake on that long trip after having had so little sleep if I wasn't there to help him? What if he had to jam on the brakes suddenly in all that traffic and the truck jackknifed?

I begged and pleaded with him not to go. I cried and yelled and did everything I could to convince him not to go. He went anyway saying he had to take care of his family and this was the only thing he could do.

As soon as he walked out the door, I heard the Lord say deep in my heart, "Give him to me. He's mine." I immediately knew this was a cross experience that was allowed by God to kill the idolatry in my heart related to my deep love for my husband. I asked God for his assurance that he would be safe. God gave me chapter and verse to look up. It was Isaiah 43:2,

> When thou passest through the waters, I will be with thee; and through the rivers, they shall not overflow thee: when thou walkest through the fire, thou shalt not be burned; neither shall the flame kindle upon thee. (Isa:43:2)

God, in his gentle, kind, loving way, had assured me that he would protect my husband, and yet in spite of God's promise there was a deep, literally physical pain in my heart. I knew it was crucifixion. I knew I was dying to Stoner so I just let God do his work. I went back to bed and cried all day… something I had never done before nor have I since. (I'm not a person prone to depression.) By cooperating with God, the whole thing was over quickly.

This whole situation would not have accomplished anything spiritual if I had not understood the concept of the working of the cross in a Christian's life. I could have worried all day, been angry at Stoner for going, and basically indulged in a lot of sinful attitudes. By not fighting and allowing God to do his work, it was over quickly and I had greater freedom to enjoy God and my husband. It is the cross that sets us free, and yet few Christians understand this basic foundational understanding of the ways of God.

God has wonderful rewards for his faithful ones even as the terrible judgments upon the wicked are going on all around us. The greatest reward is the coming of his presence to us personally. The John the Baptist Company, those who were prepared to minister to the church in the end times, have been raised up by God into a very high place of his presence. It is God's intention that all those who received their ministry also rise up into this same high place. Then they in turn will go forth and minister to others and help them rise up also. In this way the kingdom of God will come on earth. We see the ones who received the ministry of the witnesses in the first verse of the next chapter in Revelation. They are depicted as the woman who is a wonder in heaven. The ministry of the two witnesses has helped the church, the woman, also rise up into this high place.

The nations are angry because they want to control everyone and rule the world. They have been laying plans for this for centuries. And now there are these Christians who not only say God reigns over the earth but they also have his miraculous power, and they refuse to follow anyone but God.

Let's look at some of these groups who are angry now because God is raising up his people who pose a real threat to their plans to rule the world themselves. All their plans that have developed over centuries are now in danger of being foiled. Anyone who has researched the Illuminati knows that they have been working towards world domination for centuries with plans to control all the people of the world including all the world's money, food supply, religions, infrastructures and governments. Then there are the Muslims who want to take over the world for Allah, and have their Sharia law instituted all over the world. According to the research I've done, the billionaire bankers, part of the Illuminati, are the ones behind the scenes running things. The politicians we see who seem to be in charge and making decisions are only puppets in the hands of the elite bankers who, in the natural appear to be the ones really in control. But, of course, they are being controlled by deceitful demons and it all ultimately leads straight to the Devil who has already been defeated by Jesus.

Destroying the Earth

Part of the judgment God will bring on the earth will involve destroying them that destroy the earth. At the time Revelation was written, I don't believe it was possible for human beings to even conceive of anyone destroying the earth. Now it is actually happening. It is amazing to see the many ways human beings can think of to destroy this perfect, beautiful earth God created.

Genetic engineering, where a gene from the DNA of one species is injected into the DNA of another species, is totally ruining plant and animal life. The plants they've engineered do grow but their seeds, if they have any, do not produce any good fruit. This places humanity at the mercy of those who control the seeds. These genetically engineered plants cross pollinate to infest all the similar plants in a given area thereby polluting all the plants and making them barren. The chemicals that are put on these fields cause a reaction that results in the creation of super-weeds and super-bugs. When man tries to change God's creation for evil purposes, it gets out of hand and results in uncontrollable disaster.

They are doing this with food products including corn, soy, canola, papaya, sugarbeets and tomatoes among many others. Also some animals are being genetically altered...salmon for example. They are changing our food genetically and, here in America, are not required by law to tell us what they are doing to the food we eat. This should be a strong indication as to where the hearts of our congressional representatives lie. It is a fairly easy trace to track congressional decision making back to big business such as oil, pharmaceutical, and chemical.

We need to read labels to avoid eating foods we know are most likely to have been genetically altered. God made our bodies to ingest plants and animals with the specific DNA he placed in them. It has been scientifically proven that many GM foods have a deleterious effect on the human body. Now that these fundamentals of creation have been changed, the health of all humanity and the food supply of the entire world is endangered.

Then there is the whole matter of pollution. There is an area of plastic garbage twice the size of Texas floating in the Pacific Ocean (CNN). The problem is plastic doesn't bio-degrade, it photo-degrades, a process where it is broken down by sunlight into smaller pieces but they still remain plastics. Our plastic trash goes into the oceans. It gets eaten by smaller life forms that are eaten by larger forms until eventually it winds up in our dinner in the form of chemicals that endanger our health. Eating this plastic is associated with early onset diabetes, problems with liver, kidneys, etc and has become a major threat to human health. The chemicals from these plastics in our food can also cause infertility.

If that is not scary enough, there is radioactive pollution from thousands of nuclear tests combined with nuclear power plant disasters and depleted uranium weaponry used in wars such as Iraq and Afghanistan that is making large portions of our earth uninhabitable according to geoscientist Leuren Moret and others.

The problem of radiation pollution goes virtually unmentioned by our government or the media and yet incidences of diabetes, cancer, and infertility caused from radiation poisoning are becoming epidemic. The World Health Organization, according to an article and video posted on CNN Health, estimates that cancer incidences will increase 57% in the next two decades (Hume and Christensen).

The above mentioned article is very interesting because if we are discerning, we can see that they present a problem (one most likely to cause fear), but blame it on the wrong reason… an aging population… a group the One World Order wants to wipe out (Day). Then they claim this will be a burden that will damage world economies. (The word "burden" is in the article several times.) And, of course, it is unfair to poor countries… unfairness being one of their favorite mantras to bring prosperous nations down to the level of third world countries that will be easier to control. Please see the quote below:

> The rising incidence of cancer, brought about chiefly by growing, aging populations worldwide, will require a heavier focus on preventive public health policies, said Christopher Wild, director of the International Agency for Research on Cancer.

The report notes that the rocketing cost of responding to the "cancer burden" -- in 2010, the economic cost of the disease worldwide was estimated at $1.16 trillion -- is hurting the economies of rich countries and beyond the means of poor ones.

This is really strange because anyone in the public health field at the world level should be aware of the ever-increasing levels of radiation all over our world. Radiation is probably the single most causative factor in the development of malignancies which are increasing worldwide in all age groups not just the elderly.

"The International Journal of Environmental Research and Public Health" has just published an epidemiological study, entitled "Cancer, Infant Mortality and Birth Sex-Ratio in Fallujah, Iraq" stating among other things that Fallujah is experiencing higher rates of cancer, leukemia and infant mortality than Hiroshima and Nagasaki did in 1945. According to independent scientist Leuren Moret, the depleted uranium used in U.S. weaponry since 1991, has irradiated every Middle Eastern country our nation has invaded since that date (Moret).

As of the writing of this book in 2014, the tsunami of 2011 that damaged the Fukushima Daiichi nuclear power plant in Japan has resulted in tons of radioactive water being poured into the Pacific Ocean on a daily basis. Also plumes of radiation are still escaping into the atmosphere. The currents of the ocean and air transport this radioactivity towards Hawaii, Alaska and the United States mainland as well as other places. The whole world is being made uninhabitable. No one knows how to stop the flow of radiation coming from these decimated reactors (Moret).

As Christians we must take comfort in the fact that God promises us a new heaven and a new earth (2 Pet 3:13, Rev 21:1). Until then we find our health, strength and provision from his hand. We must dwell in the secret place of the Most High under the shadow of the Almighty. Our God is able and he will help us.

Verse and Interpretation

Rev 11:18 And the nations were angry, and thy wrath is come, and the time of the dead, that they should be judged, and that thou shouldest give reward unto thy servants the prophets, and to the saints, and them that fear thy name, small and great; and shouldest destroy them which destroy the earth.

All the nations and people groups who had wanted to rule the world themselves are angry that Almighty God is obviously the one who is ruling. This is the time of the final judgment of God's wrath upon all those on the earth who have rejected him (the dead). God will reward all those who have been faithful to him and destroy those who have rejected him and tried to destroy the earth.

* * * * * * * * *

>Rev 11:19 And the temple of God was opened in heaven, and there was seen in his temple the ark of his testament: and there were lightnings, and voices, and thunderings, and an earthquake, and great hail.

The Day of the Lord

In the previous verse, the servants, prophets and saints of God are rewarded for their faithfulness. Now this verse reveals what these rewards are. These faithful ones do not have to die and go to heaven to receive these rewards. The rewards are given by God even while they are still alive on the earth. This is the Day of the Lord which is a day of judgment. The sinners are to be removed out of the earth.

> Behold, the day of the LORD cometh, cruel both with wrath and fierce anger, to lay the land desolate: and he shall destroy the sinners thereof out of it (Isa 13:9).

But the righteous are to inherit the earth.

> For the upright shall dwell in the land, and the perfect shall remain in it. But the wicked shall be cut off from the earth, and the transgressors shall be rooted out of it (Prov 2:21, 22).

> For the day of the LORD is near upon all the heathen: as thou hast done, it shall be done unto thee: thy reward shall return upon thine own head. For as ye have drunk upon my holy mountain, so shall all the heathen drink continually, yea, they shall drink, and they shall swallow down, and they shall be as though they had not been. But upon mount Zion shall be deliverance, and there shall be holiness; and the house of Jacob shall possess their possessions (Oba 1:15-17).

The people of God have nothing to fear as the judgment of God is executed on the earth in these end times. God is allowing the heathen to do horrendous things to destroy the people of the earth and the earth itself, but those who are righteous will find provision and protection in God. The rewards we will be given will bring us into the presence of the Lord, and the curse put upon all humankind at the fall will be lifted off us. This will be a process and the ministry of the two witnesses will help the church enter into this new realm in God. The witnesses themselves entered this realm in Rev 11:11, 12, and their ministry will bring the church into this place also. This place is described in Rev 12 where the woman, a type of the church, is seen as a wonder in heaven.

The Temple Opened

Now let's look at these rewards in detail as recorded in our current verse. The first is: "And the temple of God was opened in heaven". The first question we need to ask ourselves is what is the temple? Is it a building in heaven that we will be allowed to look into? We must look to Scripture to give us our understanding, and we will find it in 1 Corinthians.

> *Know ye not that ye are the temple of God, and that the Spirit of God dwelleth in you? (1 Cor 3:16).*

This is the same temple the witnesses were to measure in the first verse of this chapter. This makes it clear that we are the temple of God. I am a temple as an individual, and we are the temple corporately as believers. If the temple is to be opened, then the temple must have been closed. What is there about us that is closed?

There is a side of our being that has been closed to us since the fall. This side of us is spiritual. When God told Adam and Eve that they would die the very day they ate of the forbidden fruit, they did die. It was not their physical body that died immediately; it was the spiritual side of their being that died immediately... their spiritual mind and their spiritual body. When we receive Jesus Christ as our Savior, our spiritual mind is quickened. However, there is a vast portion of the spiritual mind that will not be accessible to us until we come into perfection in the end times.

In this way they were cast out of the garden. The garden is a realm in God that must be accessed by holiness and spirituality. We cannot comprehend this realm so long as we have any darkness in our heart. In the spiritual realm we see according to what is in our heart. If there is any sin in our heart, we will be open to the deception of Satan and his minions. God has protected us from this realm by keeping our spiritual side "asleep" until such a time as we come into spiritual perfection.

To be perfected is to be without a carnal nature. All human beings have a carnal nature. In Christ we have been able to overcome by reckoning ourselves dead to sin and alive to God. By the cross, our sin nature is crucified but there is still a tendency towards some darkness in all of us. In these end times as the world is being judged, God is judging his church also, but this judgment is redemptive in nature. He will totally kill our sin nature that it will never rise again. Then he will be able to open the spiritual realm to us and we will have an open heaven.

People in satanic cults have allowed their spiritual side to be opened by demons. This is one reason why God forbids us to participate in any occult activities (Deut 18:10-12). These activities permit demons to open our spiritual side. Supernatural manifestations are then possible and people become addicted to these manifestations and the Devil takes them deeper and deeper into sin until they are even willing to sacrifice their own children to the Devil for more supernatural experiences and power. This goes on today on a large scale even in so-called civilized countries. Abuse is severe and rampant. Anyone with a lot of evil spiritual power is an abuser of a magnitude far worse than anyone could possibly imagine. I know about this because I minister to people who have been abused in satanic cults. In order to get free of their abuse, they must remember the abuse that has been locked away in dissociated parts. These parts must be delivered out of darkness and brought to Jesus for healing.

This is why God does not open this realm to us until we are perfected. There may be glimpses of this realm as the veil is briefly drawn aside for spiritual gifts to operate (1 Cor 12), but for the most part, we are not permitted to be in this dimension of spirituality for our own protection. There is an evil spirit realm and there is a heavenly realm. Once our spiritual eyes are opened we will be able to see into both as the Lord wills for his purpose.

So we can see here that the temple being opened in heaven can be interpreted as our spiritual side that has been closed since the fall being opened by God such that we can see into the spiritual realm. The first thing we see there is in the next clause, "and there was seen in his temple the ark of his testament."

The Ark of His Testament

I think most Bible students know that the ark is a type of Christ. So the first thing we see when heaven is opened is Jesus, the one about whom both Old and New Testaments testify. We have to be like him in order to see him because we see with our heart. Any sin in our heart will block our view of him.

> *Beloved, now are we the sons of God, and it doth not yet appear what we shall be: but we know that, when he shall appear, we shall be like him; for we shall see him as he is. And every man that hath this hope in him purifieth himself, even as he is pure (1 John 3:2, 3).*

As this passage says, if we hope to see Jesus we need to purify our hearts so we can be like him. This opening of heaven is a process. As God works in our lives and we cooperate with him by denying our self and walking in ever deepening levels of holiness, our vision of Jesus will gradually become clearer.

Lightnings, Voices and Thunderings

In addition to seeing Jesus, we will also hear him. Lightnings, voices and thunderings are not to be taken literally but figuratively regarding great disclosures of truth the Lord will give us. Flashes of spiritual insight will illumine our understanding like lightening brightens a night sky. Sometimes the Lord will give such clear revelations it will be almost as though we heard an audible voice. Thunderings represent astounding revelations that will shake our former understandings to the core.

An Earthquake

Our physical body, being made of dust or clay, is a type of the earth. Our body is literally going to quake. This is not a bad thing but a very pleasant thing. I know because it has happened to me. This is what we feel when our spiritual body is awakened by God. When our temple is opened, we not only begin to see Jesus and receive his incredible communications, but also we begin to feel him as our spiritual body is awakened. It has been my experience (which I will describe more fully below) that I cannot tell the difference between my spiritual body and my natural body. They feel like one to me.

I have only been in a real earthquake once. It was in 2008 when I was visiting in Orange County, California. Four of us were in an automobile stopped at a stoplight. Suddenly I started to feel a wavelike motion much like being on a river in a boat. The stoplight overhead started swaying. It lasted for several seconds. I thought it was incredibly exciting and was not in the least frightened. When we got back to my friend's apartment, aftershocks continued for a few hours. At those times, her ceiling fan would sway back and forth. This was a 5.4 quake that was even mentioned on the national news that evening. Even though the potential for terrible destruction was a possibility, I knew Jesus would keep us safe and the whole thing felt rather gentle.

The following describes my experience when my spiritual earth began to quake in February 1997.

My Earthquake Experience

On February 11, 1997 a close and very prophetic friend of mine had, in my presence, a vision of Jesus and me together in a lovely meadow. In the vision Jesus and I were sitting on a large rock talking. Jesus reached down and touched my feet and said, "These feet will never touch the earth again." I had no idea what that meant. (A few days prior to this she had had a vision that Jesus and I were married. I hadn't understood that one either.)

That night as I was lying in bed all relaxed and waiting for sleep to come, I began to feel a very pleasant, rhythmic, tingling sensation in my feet that worked its way up my legs and spread out over my entire body. I immediately related it to the vision earlier that day where Jesus touched my feet and said they would never touch the earth again.

Due to the things that the Holy Spirit was showing me in his Word, I was aware that I had not only a physical body but also a spiritual body that I would live in when I no longer needed my earthly body. I knew this spiritual body was with me but was in a dormant state as though asleep. As I felt this gentle, wave-like movement deep inside, I knew I was feeling my spiritual body being awakened. Because it started in my feet, I immediately identified it with my friend's vision. I knew Jesus had touched me in a distinct and heretofore unknown way. It was a personal and most wonderful experience which is difficult to describe. The feeling has never left but has only intensified. Because this is a spiritual experience, it is difficult to describe in words. Now I understand why so much of the Bible is written as allegory. There would be no other way to explain spiritual things except by relating them to natural things we understand.

Now I understand why there was a previous vision of Jesus and me being married. It was leading up to the experience I describe here that would come a few days later. This is one of the events of the second coming of Christ. It is an experience for his bride. I was allowed to have this experience earlier than others so I could see it in the Word as I study and then write books and record videos to help others understand when it happens to them.

I will attempt to describe the feeling of the spiritual body being awakened by Jesus. It is a very gentle, slow rhythmic feeling almost like a deep massage but it doesn't touch the skin. It is deep inside and it gives the feeling of being deeply loved. Every fiber of my being feels loved. It is like bobbing up and down on a raft resting upon gentle waves like one would experience in a bay perhaps or one of the Great Lakes. Ocean waves would be too strong. These are gentle waves. They never, ever stop…not for one second. I cannot tell my physical body from my spiritual body because my whole being feels this wonderful sense of God's love and quickening. It is deeply relaxing and comforting.

I know I am never alone because I am able to feel God's love at all times. It is a most wonderful and amazing experience and a necessary one for what we are about to experience as the Antichrist spirit begins his overt attempt to take over the world. No matter what is going on around us, this knowledge that we are loved and we are not alone never leaves.

It also brings an understanding that we have entered into a supernatural realm. Things will never be the same. Part of us has risen above the earthly realm and heaven is very near. This is the realm we will need to live in as our world crumbles around us.

We know by this event that we are in the end times. This is not something experienced by the saints of bygone years. This is a new experience and one reserved for this particular time in history. It is part of the events of the return of Jesus for his bride. God never does things the way we think he will. This experience came as a total surprise to me.

Great Hail

After I had this experience of my spiritual side being awakened by Jesus, I found the Bible opening to me as never before. I still spent hours a day studying and checking each word in the concordance to determine its meaning in the Hebrew or Greek language, but the results of my studies were yielding deeper revelations than I had previously known. This is where "great hail" may be explained.

We know that the Bible is referred to in Ephesians as being the water of the word. Frozen water from the natural heavens is called "hail." Hail melts shortly after it comes to earth. One could not wash in hail or drink it unless it had first melted. Hail represents portions of the Bible that have been impossible to understand until thawed out by the Holy Spirit in the end times when it is time for the church to know certain things that were previously not to be known.

There are certain things that the church of previous ages was not permitted to know because it was not time for them to enter into them. The awakening of the spiritual body would be one of those things reserved for the church of the end times. These truths for the end times have been in the Scriptures all along, but their true meaning could not be disclosed until it was time for the church to enter into these things.

I could never have seen what I see in the Word before my spiritual body and mind were awakened. This awakening happened as a distinct event as described above; however, there is also a gradual awakening and maturing that occurs as a process. When my spiritual body was awakened, I became aware that I could feel Jesus' touch. I also learned that he communicated with me via touch.

Over the years, his touch has become more and more perceptible to me. Also he speaks more often now and in more detail than at first. When he wants to reassure me that something I'm thinking is true or right, I'll feel gentle warmth like the sun shining on my face. If I think a thought that is not true, my nose will suddenly tickle and I'll sneeze. If I start to say something he does not want me to say, my voice will suddenly become hoarse and gravelly. No matter how much I try to clear my throat, it will not clear until I stop saying what I'm not to say. These are only a few of the many ways he speaks to me via my body. This is part of the way he refines us in all the little details in preparation for coming into perfection.

This is a way of speaking that cannot be faked by the enemy. I have the thought and immediately the feeling comes. Otherwise if a thought came into my mind like a voice or strong thought from some other entity, it could possibly be coming from a demon or possibly from extremely low frequency (ELF) waves being beamed at me from some satellite or cell tower. If this strains your credulity, you are not alone. However, we need to be aware there are technological weapons of mind control that are not yet known to the general public. There are books, Internet talk shows and online videos in abundance on this subject. Some of the best I have found are by Dr. John Hall and Dr. Robert Duncan.

When our spiritual side is awakened, that does not mean we have arrived at perfection. However, I do believe it requires a certain level of maturity before we experience this. If we had a lot of darkness in our heart when our spiritual side was awakened, we would be more open to demonic presences that could frighten or deceive us. The awakening of our spiritual side enables us to hear from the Lord in great detail. He uses this to bring us into ever deepening levels of holiness, perfection and relationship.

Verse and Interpretation

Rev 11:19 And the temple of God was opened in heaven, and there was seen in his temple the ark of his testament: and there were lightnings, and voices, and thunderings, and an earthquake, and great hail.

With the coming of maturity (previous verses) the believers (temple) are permitted to see into the heavenly realm (opened in heaven). There within (in his temple) they see Jesus (the ark) who is just like his Word says he is (of his testament). Jesus communicates with them in many ways that bring great disclosures of truth and understanding (lightnings, voices, thunderings). Their spiritual side that has been sleeping is awakened (earthquake) and portions of the Word reserved for the church of the end times are revealed to them (hail).

* * * * * * * * *

This interpretation of Revelation 11 flows perfectly into the next chapter, Revelation 12. In Revelation 12, the woman, seen as a wonder in heaven, represents the church of the end times who has come up to a higher spiritual dimension in Christ as a result of the anointed, powerful ministry of the two witnesses. In this chapter, as a result of her position in Christ, she uses the weapons of warfare Christ has given her that gives power to Michael and his angels to prevail against Satan and his angels and cast them out of their evil heavenly realm.

Appendix I

Verses and Interpretations
Revelation 11

Rev 11:1 And there was given me a reed like unto a rod: and the angel stood, saying, Rise, and measure the temple of God, and the altar, and them that worship therein.

There are persons who have received a call from God to go forth and preach in the churches. They are told that their words will measure the hearts of the people both corporately and individually. Persons will have to decide whether or not they are willing to die to self in order to follow Christ.

Rev 11:2 But the court which is without the temple leave out, and measure it not; for it is given unto the Gentiles: and the holy city shall they tread under foot forty and two months.

Don't go into the outer court church to preach. It has been given to the unbelievers who have rejected the true gospel. They will persecute the true church during the time of the Antichrist until the Lord comes.

Rev 11:3 And I will give power unto my two witnesses, and they shall prophesy a thousand two hundred and three-score days, clothed in sackcloth.

I will give power to my two witnesses, the Holy Spirit and those who are preparing the way for the second coming of Christ. They will preach my word during the period of time marked by the Antichrist spirit. They will be clothed in humility.

> Rev 11:4 *These are the two olive trees, and the two candlesticks standing before the God of the earth.*

(a) The ministries filled with the Holy Spirit that are called to prepare the church for the second coming of Christ have an unceasing anointing continually flowing forth. (b) Their spiritual mind united with the mind of Christ is a lamp that exposes what is in people's hearts. (c) Whatever they say will be enforced by Almighty God because they are speaking God's words not their own.

> Rev 11:5 *And if any man will hurt them, fire proceedeth out of their mouth, and devoureth their enemies: and if any man will hurt them, he must in this manner be killed.*

And if any false doctrine (man) tries to harm the ministry coming forth from the anointed ministers in the John the Baptist Company (them,) the fiery, anointed words (fire) coming out of their mouths (proceedeth) will destroy (devour) these false doctrines (their enemies). Any false belief (man) that tries to harm the ministry (hurt them) will be killed in this manner.

> Rev 11:6 *These have power to shut heaven, that it rain not in the days of their prophecy: and have power over waters to turn them to blood, and to smite the earth with all plagues, as often as they will.*

The John the Baptist Company of ministers filled with the Holy Spirit (These) will have the power to withhold blessings from the lives of persons who oppose their teaching in order that the people can go through difficult experiences that will reveal to them that their doctrine, when put to the test, is actually false (power to shut heaven that it rain not). At the same time they are experiencing these difficulties, the ministers, by their preaching, will be bringing the Scriptures (water) to life for them (blood). Those who oppose the teachings may also suffer physical afflictions until they are ready to discard their false doctrines and receive the truth as taught by the witnesses.

> Rev 11:7 *And when they shall have finished their testimony, the beast that ascendeth out of the bottomless pit shall make war against them, and shall overcome them, and kill them.*

When the time comes determined by God that the witnesses have completed the task God assigned them, then the law of sin will rise up out of the carnal sin nature within some of the church people to oppose the ministry, drive the ministers out of the established church and thereby kill the ministry.

> Rev 11:8 And their dead bodies shall lie in the street of the great city, which spiritually is called Sodom and Egypt, where also our Lord was crucified.

The ministry to prepare the way of the Lord (Their) seems to be a failure (dead bodies) in the wide, broad way (street) of the church (the great city) that is spiritually corrupted by sin reminiscent of Sodom and by worldly influences (Egypt). The church leaders kill the present day ministry in the church similarly to the way the religious leaders killed Jesus in their attempts to stop his ministry (where also our Lord was crucified).

> Rev 11:9 And they of the people and kindreds and tongues and nations shall see their dead bodies three days and an half, and shall not suffer their dead bodies to be put in graves.

This upheaval in the established churches is going on all over the world. It can be known by everyone because of the worldwide electronic media and also because of the gossip of local people. The remains of the ministry are visible… the books, CDs, videos, buildings, etc. and also the changed lives of the people. This continues for the period of time necessary to bring completion of separation between the true believers who received the ministry and those who rejected it. When the churches separate because of this powerful ministry, those who opposed the ministry won't drop the issue but keep it ongoing with their gossip.

> Rev 11:10 And they that dwell upon the earth shall rejoice over them, and make merry, and shall send gifts one to another; because these two prophets tormented them that dwelt on the earth.

The people who have chosen to live a worldly life of satisfying their own selfish lusts and who have joined with like-minded others to oppose this ministry rejoice that their conscience will no longer prick them now that the ministry is finished.

> *Rev 11:11 And after three days and an half the Spirit of life from God entered into them, and they stood upon their feet; and great fear fell upon them which saw them.*

When the time was completed (three) whereby everyone concerned had had the opportunity to choose for or against the ministry which was the same as choosing for or against God (half – divided), the Spirit of life from God entered into the ministry. The ministry arose in power causing those who had rejected it to realize they had been wrong and that there would be consequences for this.

> *Rev 11:12 And they heard a great voice from heaven saying unto them, Come up hither. And they ascended up to heaven in a cloud; and their enemies beheld them. And God called them up to a high spiritual realm (come up hither) where he dwells (heaven) and the presence and glory of God came upon them (cloud). This was observed by all who had opposed them including the demonic realm.*

> *Rev 11:13 And the same hour was there a great earthquake, and the tenth part of the city fell, and in the earthquake were slain of men seven thousand: and the remnant were affrighted, and gave glory to the God of heaven.*

At the same time as the witnesses ascend up to a higher realm in God and the glory of God comes upon them, a worldwide disaster will strike. This disaster will cause all in the church that falls short of the perfection of divine order to fall. What people think are spiritually perfect understandings will die – trusted doctrines and ministries based in false beliefs will all fall. The people in the church who have not opposed the John the Baptist Company will be frightened, and yet they will still give glory to God in heaven.

Verse and Interpretation

> *Rev 11:14 The second woe is past; and, behold, the third woe cometh quickly.*

The ministry of judging the church is past, and very soon the Devil will be cast out of the heavenly realm onto the earth and cause great grief to all the inhabitants of the earth and sea.

> Rev 11:15 And the seventh angel sounded; and there were great voices in heaven, saying, The kingdoms of this world are become the kingdoms of our Lord, and of his Christ; and he shall reign for ever and ever.

A message comes forth (angel sounded) that it is time for people to come into spiritual perfection (seventh). This is coming from the ministers whose ministry died and was resurrected (voices in heaven). They are calling the remnant of the church that was judged to come into perfection that the kingdom of God can come on the earth as it is in heaven.

> Rev 11:16 And the four and twenty elders, which sat before God on their seats, fell upon their faces, and worshipped God,

And their spiritual minds in governmental perfection (24 elders) which had come into rest (sat) and abode in the presence of God (before God) were continuously worshiping God and enjoying his presence.

> Rev 11:17 Saying, We give thee thanks, O Lord God Almighty, which art, and wast, and art to come; because thou hast taken to thee thy great power, and hast reigned

The witnesses in their spiritual minds were able to thank God for all things because they recognized his Almightiness manifested in all of life (Almighty God) including the present (which art), the past (and wast) and the future (art to come). They could see that God's power had worked all things together for good and his sovereign will had been accomplished in every aspect of their lives.

> Rev 11:18 And the nations were angry, and thy wrath is come, and the time of the dead, that they should be judged, and that thou shouldest give reward unto thy servants the prophets, and to the saints, and them that fear thy name, small and great; and shouldest destroy them which destroy the earth.

All the nations and people groups who had wanted to rule the world themselves are angry that Almighty God is obviously the one who is ruling. This is the time of the final judgment upon the earth. God is rewarding all those who have been faithful to him and destroying those who have rejected him and tried to destroy the earth.

Interpretations Only

Revelation 11

Rev 11:1

There are persons who have received a call from God to go forth and preach in the churches. They are told that their words will measure the hearts of the people both corporately and individually. Persons will have to decide whether or not they are willing to die to self in order to follow Christ.

Rev 11:2

Don't go into the outer court church to preach. It has been given to the unbelievers who have rejected the true gospel. They will persecute the true church during the time of the Antichrist until the Lord comes.

Rev 11:3

I will give power to my two witnesses, the Holy Spirit and those who are preparing the way for the second coming of Christ. They will preach my word during the period of time marked by the Antichrist spirit. They will be clothed in humility.

Rev 11:4

The ministries filled with the Holy Spirit that are called to prepare the church for the second coming of Christ have an unceasing anointing continually flowing forth. Their spiritual mind united with the mind of Christ is a lamp that exposes what is in people's hearts. Whatever they say will be enforced by Almighty God because they are speaking God's words not their own.

Rev 11:5

And if any false doctrine (man) tries to harm the ministry coming forth from the anointed ministers in the John the Baptist Company (them,) the fiery, anointed words (fire) coming out of their mouths (proceedeth) will destroy (devour) these false doctrines (their enemies). Any false belief (man) that tries to harm the ministry (hurt them) will be killed in this manner.

Rev 11:6

The John the Baptist Company of ministers filled with the Holy Spirit (These) will have the power to withhold blessings from the lives of persons who oppose their teaching in order that the people can go through difficult experiences that will reveal to them that their doctrine, when put to the test, is actually false (power to shut heaven that it rain not). At the same time they are experiencing these difficulties, the ministers, by their preaching, will be bringing the Scriptures (water) to life for them (blood). Those who oppose the teachings may also suffer physical afflictions until they are ready to discard their false doctrines and receive the truth as taught by the witnesses.

Rev 11:7

When the time comes determined by God that the witnesses have completed the task God assigned them, then the law of sin will rise up out of the carnal sin nature within some of the church people to oppose the ministry, drive the ministers out of the established church and thereby kill the ministry.

Rev 11:8

The ministry to prepare the way of the Lord (Their) seems to be a failure (dead bodies) in the wide, broad way (street) of the church (the great city) that is spiritually corrupted by sin reminiscent of Sodom and by worldly influences (Egypt). The church leaders kill the present day ministry in the church similarly to the way the religious leaders killed Jesus in their attempts to stop his ministry (where also our Lord was crucified).

Rev 11:9

This upheaval in the established churches is going on all over the world. It can be known by everyone because of the worldwide electronic media and also because of the gossip of local people. The remains of the ministry are visible… the books, CDs, videos, buildings, etc. and also the changed lives of the people. This continues for the period of time necessary to bring completion of separation between the true believers who received the ministry and those who rejected it. When the churches separate because of this powerful ministry, those who opposed the ministry won't drop the issue but keep it ongoing with their gossip.

Rev 11:10

The people who have chosen to live a worldly life of satisfying their own selfish lusts and who have joined with like-minded others to oppose this ministry rejoice that their conscience will no longer prick them now that the ministry is finished.

Rev 11:11

When the time was completed (three) whereby everyone concerned had had the opportunity to choose for or against the ministry which was the same as choosing for or against God (half – divided), the Spirit of life from God entered into the ministry. The ministry arose in power causing those who had rejected it to realize they had been wrong and that there would be consequences for this.

Rev 11:12

And God called them up to a high spiritual realm (come up hither) where he dwells (heaven) and the presence and glory of God came upon them (cloud). This was observed by all who had opposed them including the demonic realm.

Rev 11:13

At the same time as the witnesses ascend up to a higher realm in God and the glory of God comes upon them, a worldwide disaster will strike. This disaster will cause all in the church that falls short of the perfection of divine order to fall. What people think are spiritually perfect understandings will die – trusted doctrines and ministries based in false beliefs will all fall. The people in the church who have not opposed the John the Baptist Company will be frightened, and yet they will still give glory to God in heaven.

Rev 11:14

The ministry of judging the church is past, and very soon the Devil will be cast out of the heavenly realm onto the earth and cause great grief to all the inhabitants of the earth and sea.

Rev 11:15

A message comes forth (angel sounded) that it is time for people to come into spiritual perfection (seventh). This is coming from the ministers whose ministry died and was resurrected (voices in heaven). They are calling the remnant of the church that was judged to come into perfection that the kingdom of God can come on the earth as it is in heaven.

Rev 11:16

And their spiritual minds in governmental perfection (24 elders) which had come into rest (sat) and abode in the presence of God (before God) were continuously worshiping God and enjoying his presence.

Rev 11:17

The witnesses in their spiritual minds were able to thank God for all things because they recognized his Almightiness manifested in all of life (Almighty God) including the present (which art), the past (and wast) and the future (art to come). They could see that God's power had worked all things together for good and his sovereign will had been accomplished in every aspect of their lives.

Rev 11:18

All the nations and people groups who had wanted to rule the world themselves are angry that Almighty God is obviously the one who is ruling. This is the time of the final judgment upon the earth. God is rewarding all those who have been faithful to him and destroying those who have rejected him and tried to destroy the earth.

Appendix II

Bible Study Questions

Revelation 11

Context: The last verse of the previous chapter states:

Rev 10:11 And he said unto me, Thou must prophesy again before many peoples, and nations, and tongues, and kings. (Prophesy can mean to foretell events but it can also mean to preach.) This is our lead-in clue to understanding the next verse.

Rev 11:1 And there was given me a reed like unto a rod: and the angel stood, saying, Rise, and measure the temple of God, and the altar, and them that worship therein.

- Reed is *kalamos* in Greek. It means "a pen." (see Psalm 45:1)
- Rod – something used for measuring
- What is the temple of God? Is it a building? (1 Cor 3:16)
- What does the altar represent? (Luke 9:23-27)

Rev 11:2 *But the court which is without the temple leave out, and measure it not; for it is given unto the Gentiles: and the holy city shall they tread under foot forty and two months.*

- Based on your understanding of what a temple is, what would "the court which is without" represent?
- What would Gentiles represent?
- What is the holy city? Is it Jerusalem or is it something spiritual?
- What does the number "42" represent? (E.W. Bullinger's book *Number in Scripture* can be viewed free online at http://philologos.org/__eb-nis/default.htm

Rev 11:3 *And I will give power unto my two witnesses, and they shall prophesy a thousand two hundred and three-score days, clothed in sackcloth.*

- Who are the witnesses? See John 15:26. Luke 1:76, John 1:6, 7. Remember, individuals in the Bible are often representative of groups of people in contemporary life.

- What does 1,260 days represent spiritually? (Break it down into months.)
- What does sackcloth represent spiritually?
- Other scriptures related to this verse - 1 John 2:18, I John 2:22, 1 John 4:3, 2 John 1:7

Rev 11:4 These are the two olive trees, and the two candlesticks standing before the God of the earth.

- What do we get from olives? What does it represent?
- What are trees? See Luke 3:9.
- What do candlesticks represent? See Prov 20:27
- What does it mean to stand before the God of the earth? See 1 Kings 17:1

Rev 11:5 And if any man will hurt them, fire proceedeth out of their mouth, and devoureth their enemies: and if any man will hurt them, he must in this manner be killed.

- Man – The word "man" is not in the Greek. It is just understood here. According to some of the early Church Fathers, "men" can represent allegorically the understanding.
- Who are them? The witnesses themselves? The message they preach? See Luke 10:16.
- What does the fire represent? See Jer 5:14 and John 12:48.
- Who are their enemies? Eph 6:12
- See Mal 3:1-5 and Matt 13:40-42

Rev 11:6 (a) These have power to shut heaven, that it rain not in the days of their prophecy: (b) and have power over waters to turn them to blood, (c) and to smite the earth with all plagues, as often as they will.

Part (a)

- What does heaven represent here?

  Check the definition for heaven in Strong's

  Read Hosea 6:1-3

- Why do you think the witnesses would want to shut up heaven?

Part (b)
- What does water represent? See Eph 5:26
- What does blood represent? See Deut 12:23
- What do you think power over waters to turn them to blood represents?

Part (c)
- What does the earth represent here? See Gen 2:7
- What are plagues? Look up in Hebrew.
- What do you think part (c) is saying?

Rev 11:7 And when they shall have finished their testimony, the beast that ascendeth out of the bottomless pit shall make war against them, and shall overcome them, and kill them.

- Can the Holy Spirit be killed?
- Do you think God will allow a beast to kill all his witnesses?
- What is the beast?

See Rev 13. The key verses for identifying the beast are Rev 13:3 and Rom 7:8.9.

Remember numbers are not literal but spiritual.

- Do you think the beast is killing the people literally or killing their testimony?
- What is the bottomless pit?
- Could the beast be working through other people?

Rev 11:8 And their dead bodies shall lie in the street of the great city, which spiritually is called Sodom and Egypt, where also our Lord was crucified.

- Dead - Look in Strong's concordance. How many Greek words do you see that can be translated "dead" or "death?" Look up each word to see its meaning. How is the word 4430. *ptoma, pto'-mah* used here slightly different from the others? See where else in your Bible

4430. *ptoma, pto'-mah* is used. Does its usage there imply anything to you?
- What is great city?
- What does Sodom represent? (Gen 13:13)
- What does Egypt represent?
- What group was mainly responsible for Jesus' crucifixion?

Rev 11:9 And they of the people and kindreds and tongues and nations shall see their dead bodies three days and an half, and shall not suffer their dead bodies to be put in graves.

- What is the scope of the happening described here?
- What do you think the dead bodies represent (keeping in mind the slight variance in the definition for *ptoma* seen in previous verse)?
- If you think of "three" as meaning something that is completed, and if you think of "half" as meaning something separated, what do you think this means. (Hint: This has to do with "measuring the temple" as seen in the first verse.)
- What can this mean if we aren't talking about a literal dead body?

Rev 11:10 And they that dwell upon the earth shall rejoice over them, and make merry, and shall send gifts one to another; because these two prophets tormented them that dwelt on the earth.

- Why do you think people would rejoice over this?
- How did the prophets torment them?

Rev 11:11 And after three days and an half the Spirit of life from God entered into them, and they stood upon their feet; and great fear fell upon them which saw them.

- What is the spiritual meaning of three?
- Half = division
- Why were the people fearful?

Rev 11:12 And they heard a great voice from heaven saying unto them, Come up hither. And they ascended up to heaven in a cloud; and their enemies beheld them.

- Where is heaven?
- What is the cloud: (2 Chron 5:13, 14)
- Who are their enemies?

Rev 11:13 And the same hour was there a great earthquake, and the tenth part of the city fell, and in the earthquake were slain of men seven thousand: and the remnant were affrighted, and gave glory to the God of heaven.

- What do you think the earthquake might be?
- What does ten mean spiritually? Knowing this, what would a tenth part be?
- What is the city? (1 Pet 4:17)
- What do men represent here?
- What does seven mean spiritually? (The zeros of thousand represent an intensity of the number seven)
- Who do you think the remnant represents?
- What are they feeling?
- What is their response to all this?

Rev 11:14 The second woe is past; and, behold, the third woe cometh quickly.

- What was the first woe? (Rev 9)
- What is the third woe? (Rev 12)

Rev 11:15 And the seventh angel sounded; and there were great voices in heaven, saying, The kingdoms of this world are become the kingdoms of our Lord, and of his Christ; and he shall reign for ever and ever.

- What does the number seven represent spiritually?
- Whose voices do you think are speaking here from heaven.
- To whom do you think they are speaking?

Rev 11:16 And the four and twenty elders, which sat before God on their seats, fell upon their faces, and worshipped God,

(Remember this is inward not outward – Luke 17:20b, 21: The kingdom of God cometh not with observation: Neither shall they say, Lo here! or, lo there! for, behold, the kingdom of God is within you.)

- What do the twenty-four elders represent? (24 is the number of heavenly government)
- Elders = men = certain minds = ?
- Where is heaven?
- Eph 2:6 And hath raised us up together, and made us sit together in heavenly places in Christ Jesus.
- What might "sat on their seats" represent spiritually? (Heb 4:3)
- What character quality do you see demonstrated here?

Rev 11:17 Saying, We give thee thanks, O Lord God Almighty, which art, and wast, and art to come; because thou hast taken to thee thy great power, and hast reigned.

- What do you think they are understanding that enables them to see God as one who is, who was, and is to come?

Rev 11:18 And the nations were angry, and thy wrath is come, and the time of the dead, that they should be judged, and that thou shouldest give reward unto thy servants the prophets, and to the saints, and them that fear thy name, small and great; and shouldest destroy them which destroy the earth.

- Look up the word "nations" in Greek. What people could it represent here?
- Who are the dead?
- Who is being rewarded?
- Who is destroying the earth?

Rev 11:19 And the temple of God was opened in heaven,

and there was seen in his temple the ark of his testament: and there were lightnings, and voices, and thunderings, and an earthquake, and great hail.

- What do you think the temple represents?
- What do you think the ark represents?
- What do you think the following represent?

Lightnings

Voices

Thunderings

Earthquake

Great hail

Credits

Andersen, Kirsten. *http://www.lifesitenews.com/news/the-number-of-children-living-in-single-parent-homes-has-nearly-doubled-in* (accessed March 26, 2014).

Bullinger, E. W. 1067. *Number in Scripture.* Grand Rapids: Kregel Publications

Busby, Hamdan, Ariabi. 2010. *http://www.mdpi.com/1660-4601/7/7/2828.* (accessed March 29, 2014).

CNN Headline News. n.d. *https://www.youtube.com/watch?v=z7rNYzSH-BA* (accessed March 31, 2014).

Day, Lorraine M.D. n.d. *http://www.goodnewsaboutgod.com/studies/political/population_control/population_control.htm* (accessed March 29, 2014)

Gesenius, H. W. F. 1979. *Gesenius' Hebrew-Chaldea Lexicon to the Old Testament.* Grand Rapids: Baker Book House Co.

Hume and Christensen, Feb 4, 2014. "WHO: Imminent global cancer 'disaster' reflects aging, lifestyle factors." *http://www.cnn.com/2014/02/04/health/who-world-cancer-report/index.html* (accessed March 29, 2014).

Jukes, Andrew. 1976. *Types in Genesis.* Grand Rapids: Kregel Publications. Originally published 1898. London: Longmans, Green and Co.

Moret, Leuren. July 2004. *The Journal of International Issues.* "The Trojan Horse of Nuclear War." Available at *http://www.mindfully.org/Nucs/2004/DU-Trojan-Horse1jul04.htm*

June 2011. Available at *https://www.youtube.com/watch?v=2zL3M3kvgIo* (accessed Mar 8, 2014).

Thomas, Major W. Ian. 1961. *The Saving Life of Christ.* Zondervan Publishing House. Grand Rapids.

USA Today. Available at *http://www.usatoday.com/story/weather/2014/02/13/snow-cover-usa/5454645/* (accessed Mar 8, 2014).

Wigington. n.d. Available from *http://www.geoengineeringwatch.org/* (accessed March 8, 2014).

January 2014. *https://www.youtube.com/watch?v=5yZhh2leRJA* (accessed Mar 2, 2014).

wiseGEEK, n.d. http://www.wisegeek.com/what-does-radiation-do-to-living-cells.htm (accessed Mar 24, 2014).

www.ingramcontent.com/pod-product-compliance
Lightning Source LLC
Chambersburg PA
CBHW022107040426
42451CB00007B/164